If You Can't Take a Joke……

By

John R Skull

First published 2021

Copyright © John R Skull 2021

All rights reserved. No part of this book may be reproduced, stored in a retrieval system, or transmitted, in any form or by any means, electronic, mechanical, photocopying, recording or otherwise, without the prior written permission of the copyright owner.

ISBN: 979-8406116326

Cover design by Sabine Karcher ♥

Introduction

My intention in writing this book, was simply to provide a family legacy document for my children and grandchildren. I consider myself a happy survivor of what was a troubled childhood and feel that memoirs and autobiographies are the preserve of politicians, actors, rock stars and, God forbid, celebrities. This is, however, my story and tells of a Belfast childhood during the traumatic 'troubles' and the challenges of growing up in often harrowing circumstances. Many of the things that happened to others and me during my childhood, particularly in various welfare homes and borstals, were either illegal, immoral, embarrassing or downright distasteful. Part 2 tells of my decision to join the Royal Navy and the trials and tribulations of a young man who just can't seem to avoid trouble. As for the tone of the book, I would rather see the funny side of an incident than dwell upon the sadness. Of course, this does not make it un-sad. In writing and life in general, I favour comedy over drama and hugs over fists.

During my research into Bawnmore Boys' Home and Rathgael Training School, I stumbled upon the report arising from the Historical Institutional Abuse (HIA) Northern Ireland Inquiry and the subsequent HIA Compensation Scheme. I got to wondering how many others who are entitled to compensation for their harsh treatment at the hands of institutions into whose 'care' they were placed, are unaware of the Scheme. I found out by accident and I wondered if my book might also raise awareness through wider publication, rather than simply keeping it in the family, so to speak.

My hope is that the reader will chuckle more than sob, laugh at my adventures and celebrate some of my successes, rather than pity me. I also am quite intrigued as to how it will be received in fifty or a hundred years if any surviving Skulls decide to Google, Bing and Yahoo 'John Skull' they will find my story. Forgotten, but not gone!

Dedication

For my favourite daughter and her sister.

Acknowledgements

This book would not have been written without the support of my brother and sister, both of whom also endured a shoddy childhood. My wife, Sabine, was always on hand with a word of encouragement when I flagged, or a glass of whiskey when I faced the dreaded writer's block. When my artistic failings also became apparent, she stepped in and designed the cover for the book. She is awesome – always has been, always will be.

Contents

Chapter 1 – The Early Hour……………………..1

Chapter 2 – Meet the Parents…………………3

Chapter 3 – Meet the Grandparents………….10

Chapter 4 – Off to School…………………....16

Chapter 5 – Out of the Slums………………...24

Chapter 6 – From Worse to Worser………….27

Chapter 7 – Round Peg, Square Hole………...34

Chapter 8 – The Great Escape……………….41

Chapter 9 – The 'Outside'…………………....47

Chapter 10 – The System…………………….55

Chapter 11 – 'Outside' Again………………...64

Chapter 12 – Don't Try This At Home………..68

Chapter 13 – The System II………………….73

Chapter 14 – On the Inside………………….79

Chapter 15 – The Prodigal Brother Returns…87

Chapter 16 – On The Road Again…………..91

Chapter 17 – Over the Water……………….99

Chapter 18 – The Skull Family……………..108

Chapter 19 – Work Experience…………….114

Chapter 20 – Apprentices and Apprehension….123

Chapter 21 – Into the Blue……………………..126

Chapter 22 – Navy Days……………………..133

Chapter 23 – HMS GANGES………………...138

Chapter 24 – Learning the Ropes……………...144

Chapter 25 – The Run Ashore………………....149

Chapter 26 – HMS MERCURY………………159

Chapter 27 – Bunting Tosser…………………..164

Chapter 28 – HMS Juno – Oh, Dear!……………..166

Chapter 29 – The Discipline Naval Act………...172

Chapter 30 – Double Jeopardy………………...178

Chapter 31 – Life in a Blue Suit………………..183

Chapter 32 – If You Can't Take a Joke………...189

Chapter 33 – There's No 'I' in Team…………..195

Chapter 34 – War is Hell, but Colder!………….200

Chapter 35 - DOO-WAH-DIDDY-DIDDY…204

Chapter 36 – Gibraltar Sun, Sea and Sand…….211

Chapter 37 – Welcome to America Y'all!………..217

Chapter 38 – Happy 200th, America!…………...220

Chapter 39 – All Grown Up…………………...229

Epilogue - Historical Institutional Abuse (Northern Ireland)

If You Can't Take a Joke...

Chapter 1 – The Early Hours

I am fairly convinced that the foetus is more advanced than we care to imagine. I'm a twin and to this day, I remember being able to hear discussions between my parents while I was still safely ensconced in the womb. It went like this:

Mother: "Twins then. Bugger."

Father: "Bugger, indeed. What are they, then?"

Mother: "Boys, apparently."

Father: "They figure that out using some weird test on chromosomes, or something?"

Mother: "No, nothing like that. I'm carrying them low, so that means boys. What about names?"

Father: "Yeah, they ought to have names."

Mother: "What names though?"

Father: "Easy. Fred, after me and John, after your Father. But, I'm their Dad, so the first born is Fred."

Me (Inutero): "Fred, fucking Fred! John is boring, common and biblical, but fucking Fred!"

They say that twins have an uncanny knack of communicating with each other, which is beyond the capabilities and comprehension of normal people. I subscribe to this theory and I believe that the first time I communicated with my brother was in the womb, when I suggested,

"After you……Fred!"

If You Can't Take a Joke…

So, twenty minutes after Fred had been dangled by his ankles and his arse roundly slapped, I popped into the world already ahead of the game.

Chapter 2 – Meet the Parents

My recall of the early years presents some challenges, of course, due to immaturity and absorption of the memories of others. It could be that the mists of time have been further fogged by my enthusiastic enjoyment and over-medicating of whiskey as an adult - it was, after all, common practice back then to soothe a crying baby by dipping his pacifier, or dummy tit, in whiskey, so I started early.

From my earliest days, the clearest memories are of small episodes of happiness, joy and fun, squeezed between significantly larger doses of instability, alcoholism, deprivation and violence. It is not my intention to linger too long on these sad occurrences, but in the interests of the integrity of my story I shall be as candid as possible. Given the predisposition towards leniency from the justice system today, this candour may even provide useful should I ever find myself in front of a Judge, "I had a rough childhood, lack of educational opportunities and am simply the personification of the early stages of the underclass, your Honour."

Before introducing my parents, I believe a short description of Northern Ireland in the late 50s and early 60s will provide much-needed context. Belfast was still very much in the grip of post-war rebuilding, but was seemingly well behind schedule when compared to the pace of progress across the Irish Sea in England. Then again, coming over to Northern Ireland in those days was like traveling back in time about twenty years. Uncertainty about the possibility of a United Ireland seemed to instill a lack of motivation in the UK Central

Government in London, resulting in a deficiency of funding for building and infrastructure in the province. Throughout my early childhood, the feeling of a divided community was palpable, with Protestants and Catholics attending different schools, clearly defined Republican and Loyalist neighbourhoods and a general prejudice against Roman Catholics, particularly in employment opportunities. In London and across England, the Sixties became the Swinging Sixties and saw skirts getting shorter, music getting louder, men's hair getting longer and the birth of sex, drugs and rock 'n' roll! On our side of the usually choppy and grey Irish Sea we witnessed tempers getting shorter, protests getting louder, paramilitary marches getting longer and the birth of 'The Troubles'. The enduring and misguided belief that Northern Ireland's problems was a conflict between Protestants and Catholics is simply a media construct to make this complicated issue more easily digestible by the masses, but it was never about religion. The simple fact is that most of those on the Republican/Nationalist side were Roman Catholic and most of those on the Loyalist/Unionist side were Protestants. 'The Troubles' was about political power and criminal control. The Republicans wanted a United Ireland and the Loyalists wanted to remain part of the United Kingdom. In the late 1960s, the Unionists, backed by the overwhelmingly Protestant police force, disrupted the increasingly vocal Civil Rights marches and protests of the Catholics and serious rioting ensued. Once the UK government sent troops into Belfast, ironically to protect the Roman Catholics, it all went rather pear-shaped. It didn't take long for extremists on both sides to increase memberships of a number of paramilitary organisations – the most significant being the Irish Republican Army (IRA) and Irish National Liberation Army (INLA) on the Republican side and the Ulster Volunteer Force (UVF) and Ulster Defence Association (UDA) on the Loyalist side. There were offshoot groups like the Red Hand Commando (RHC), Ulster Freedom Fighters (UFF) and Loyalist Volunteer Force (LVF) and many years later I was reminded of these groups when Monty Python's Life of Brian was showing in cinemas - Popular Front of Judea, Judean Popular Front, etc.! These paramilitaries were not only embroiled in the conflict itself, but also benefited enormously from controlling most of the criminal activity and profits in areas under their control. With the escalating violence came increasing separation of communities, with a 'peace wall' being constructed between adjacent neighbourhoods - often splitting streets right down the middle. Barriers and checkpoints became the norm at all entries and exits to Belfast City centre and riots, fires, bombs, bullets and death headlined the news daily.

My parents were both from fairly typical Belfast stock of their era – raised in poverty by poorly educated, poorly motivated slum-dwellers. As a young man, my father enlisted in the Royal Irish Fusiliers, later to become the Royal Irish Rangers during one of the run of the mill efficiency drives of the late 1960s, which involved reducing costs, primarily in cap badges and stationary. He played cornet in the military band. A cornet, I'm now led to believe, is the instrument of choice for those who can't quite master the trumpet. Having been raised on a literary diet of 'tuppenny wars', the illustrated comic books of that era, I remember taking pride in telling the other guttersnipes in our street that my father was a soldier. The most popular comic of the time was called "Commando" and offered stories of escaping prisoners of war, heroic raids by outnumbered Tommies on Nazi machine gun posts and, occasionally, the escapades of maverick heroes bucking the system, only to prove that gritty common sense would prevail over the strategy of the officer class. Winning the war wasn't all that difficult, as it turns out, since the Nazi/Bosch/Hun/enemy were very poor in the field of communications, having a vocabulary limited to only a number of phrases, including,

"Gott in Himmel","Hande Hoch!" and,

"For you ze var is over, English schweinhund!"

The British Tommy, on the other hand, was square of jaw, handsome and brave and could be on-board a submarine, dropped off in a dinghy, navigate ashore, find the castle (generally at the top of a tall mountain), rescue the capture British scientist, kill a few huns and still be back home in time for breakfast with a pair of contraband silk stockings from Paris for his missus.

Like many of my early childhood friends, I fell into the 'Absent Father' status. Absent meant different things to different people. Military Service, Her Majesty's Pleasure – prison - and death all bestowed the title of 'Absent Father' on the Social Security records of the families in our street, so I took some pride in the fact that my father fell into the former category. They do say, though, that pride comes before a fall. My father was due to come back to Belfast on one of his infrequent periods of leave. In anticipation of his return, I had upped the stakes in the 'my Da is better than your Da' competition that is prevalent in childhood circles, particularly amongst young boys. I had told everyone who would care to listen, that my Father was returning from a war in Korea for a spot of R&R. I don't believe that I was making this up, but truly believed that Sergeant Wardlow was up to his nuts in the yellow peril trying to avoid having bamboo shoots shoved up his fingernails (yep, Commando again). As it happens, he was stationed in Catterick Camp, somewhere in Yorkshire, but no-one had bothered to tell me that, so I just assumed that he was off in Johnny-Foreigner-Land being heroic.

Nostalgia, or rose-tinted spectacles, would suggest that in the slums of post-war Belfast everyone looked out for each other. The truth is that everyone led such boring, uneventful and poverty-driven lives that gossip and innuendo provided the only colour in a dull and grey existence. So it was then that everyone knew to the hour when my Father was coming home. Back then, there was nothing more effective than a smart military uniform on a young man with good career prospects to guarantee the presence of all the young women of Grove Street to appear on their front doorsteps at the same time, most with snot-nosed, scruffy and greasy kids hanging around their aprons. I vividly recall my father walking smartly down the street, with a platoon of young boys marching in time behind him. I felt very proud. By the time he reached our door, he was surrounded by a score of admiring youngsters bursting with questions for the returning hero. He silenced them all with a question.

"So you want to see what I do in the Army, boys?" he asked.

He swung his Army-issue canvas kitbag off his shoulder, undid the cord securing the top and started rummaging around inside. The snot-nosed kids held their breath, awaiting the production of a Lee-Enfield .303, or at the very least a 9mm Browning pistol. Bright metal gleamed in my father's hand as he produced a cornet, not even a trumpet, a fucking cornet. Worse still, he started to play it. As musicians are wont to do, my father closed his eyes as he blared out a fair-to-middling rendition of the opening bars of Colonel Bogey. By the time he opened them, his audience had vanished and my reputation was in tatters.

My mother, a striking blonde, had an unfortunate upbringing at the hands of alcoholic and abusive parents. As a child she was removed from the family home by Social Services for a time and spent some unhappy years in a special School for Girls. To this day, my mother cannot talk about those dreadful times, but removal of children from the family home became a family theme. My mother met my father when she was sixteen and saw him not as an exciting boyfriend, a future doting husband or a loving father for her children, viewed him as an escape from the miserable, grey and violent existence of Belfast slums in the shadow of the Gallaher's cigarette factory in York Street. Marriage followed quickly and at seventeen my mother fell pregnant with my sister Caroline. Ten months later after Caroline had issued forth, Fred and I were born. A couple of years later Paul arrived, so by the time my mother was twenty one she had four children under the age of four. Adding to the woes of a young woman ill-prepared for adult life, let alone motherhood, was the fact that her youngest child Paul was severely disabled - a dwarf with a hole in his heart. It was Paul's major heart condition, more than his dwarfism, that caused him to be in and out of hospital as a child and this eventually resulted in his premature death at only 15-years old.

Chapter 3 – Meet the Grandparents

As an Army family, we followed wherever the British Government decided my father's skills were required. In my first three years, we lived in England, Germany and Libya, although what the Libyan's needed with a cornet player, I have never been able to ascertain. During this period, my mother was pretty much pregnant full time and, although I have no direct memories of this time, I know she must have been desperately unhappy. Like all the men in my mother's life to this point, my father was a violent man who applied military discipline to his family. Eventually and predictably my mother finally succumbed to the pressure and ran away. Despite what all her children now understand and accept as her only option, my mother still lives with the guilt of 'abandoning' her children to this day. My father now had to decide what to do with his four offspring, as given his occupation he was not in a position to look after us. His mother was dead and his father was very elderly. So it fell to my mother's parents to take us in. Their house was at 6 Grove Street, two streets away from the Gallaher's cigarette factory. The whole area was a collection of narrow streets of tiny smoke and smog stained Victorian slums, all owned by Belfast City Corporation and rented to the lowest socio-economic families in the area. Car ownership, particularly in the early 60's was non-existent and the streets were narrow and empty. Being so old and located quite close to the dockyard, various industrial workshops and the Gallagher's factory, the houses were coated with a thick coat of black soot and God-knows what other chemical

If You Can't Take a Joke...

concoctions. The only flash of colour cutting through the depressing greys and browns were the kerb-stones, which were painted in red, white and blue thick glossy paint, to signify to outsiders that this was a Loyalist street and none of your Fenian nonsense will be tolerated! My grandparent's house consisted of one room and a kitchen downstairs and a large room upstairs. The kitchen, or scullery as it was known in Belfast, had a door opening to the back yard. For clarity, these were definitely yards and not gardens, as never a blade of grass would be seen, just the occasional weed struggling up between uneven paving stones. The top of the walls had a layer of broken glass sticking out of cement to deter burglars and cats. At the end of the yard was the tiny toilet, with its cold, cold wooden seat and squares of cut up newspapers stuck through a wire hook, for use as toilet paper. I remember vividly the long, cold, dark, wet trek to the toilet. We all used to make a point of a visit before bedtime, as such a trip in the middle of winter was nightmarish. That horrible moment when my little Paddy arse had to make contact with the freezing wooden toilet was tinged with the belief that I could get stuck there forever, like when Joey Dunlop licked a freezing lamppost one time and had to wait ages for someone to fetch a glass of warm water to thaw both the lamppost and his tongue. A wooden gate led to the alleyway that separated the yards of the adjoining streets. On our block, there were a number of cleared areas, because of houses being bombed by the Luftwaffe, bulldozed by the council and never considered worth rebuilding. In case you are wondering about the strategic value of bombing some slum housing, I should point out that the target was

If You Can't Take a Joke...

the Belfast shipyards a couple of miles away. Back in the yard, a nail in the wall held the steel bathtub that would be brought inside once a week on bath-day. Kettles of water would be boiled and we would all be bathed in the same water. To ensure that the water would still be warm for child number four, the first child would effectively be poached and, particularly in winter, the last child would be snap frozen. We would dance around naked, trying to keep warm whilst awaiting our turn and laughing at the streaks of newsprint which appeared from between the cheeks of our little white bums. By the time we were all bathed, the water was newsprint grey, with a layer of foamy scum. Our granny hadn't mellowed since her days of abusing my mother and she was quick to beat any of us who upset her, whether by accident or ignorance. Money was always scarce and came either from occasional work in the docks for Granda, or by benefits from the Employment Bureau, the 'brew', when that work dried up. Money, whether wages or benefits, was paid on Thursdays and the major factor determining the budget for the following week was whether or not Granda passed a pub on his way home. More often than not, he did. Granny would sit on a stool outside the front door from about five o'clock on Thursday afternoon, awaiting her husband's return. This story was repeated up and down the street. At 5.30pm, the bright red hair of reliable Joey Dunlop would burst around the corner and a relieved Mrs. Dunlop would welcome him home. Shortly afterwards, Ray McCullagh would approach his wife with a spring in his step, knowing that he'd done the right thing. There would be the sound of relieved laughter from the Dunlop and

McCullagh households, while those still on the doorstep became increasingly desperate. At 6.30pm, Sean Craig would appear and tell his wife,

"Just stopped for a quick one, luv."

An obviously relieved Mrs. Craig would respond,

"Sure you've been working hard all week, darlin'. A man's entitled to pint for his efforts, so he is!"

The two or three women left on the doorsteps would be drawn together in the same desperation and eventually form a huddle of misery. It was now simply a case of how much money would be left by the time their respective husbands arrived home from the pub. Too often, my Granda would be the last to arrive and the arguing, crying and slapping would start, while we children huddled under a couple of RAF World War II greatcoats in one bed upstairs, hoping that the Granda was too inebriated for the violence to make it up the stairs.

I'm starting to feel sorry for little Johnny, so I ought to clarify how life was in Belfast in the early sixties. I'd hate anyone to think that I was surrounded by other children whose lives were all milk and honey, whilst I suffered at the hands of Dickensian grandparents. The violence of my grandparents would not have resulted in anonymous calls to Social Services. At worst, neighbours would have probably considered Granny and Granda a little 'trigger happy', but given the fact that their daughter had fucked off and lumbered them with her kids, their short-temper, alcohol abuse and quick hands were quite understandable. I find it difficult to say anything in defence of those who caused me such misery as a child, but I suppose it is important to mention that my Grandparents' generation had lived and fought through two World Wars, so violence, struggle and poverty were what moulded them, rather than opportunity, education and plenty, the fodder of the following generations, including my own. Counseling, PTSD and group-hugs hadn't been invented yet, so Granda's 'battle fatigue' - today's PTSD - and Granny's 'nerves' - anxiety or depression - went untreated and unchecked. Hardly surprising then that the only conflict resolution tools available to my Granda were alcohol and his fists of fury. The civil unrest and the 'troubles' of the following decade were busily fermenting in the slums. In fact, there were a number of Roman Catholic families in our street, but as the early sixties passed, they gradually drifted away and into Republican enclaves like the Falls Road and the New Lodge Road. The Twelfth of July would see the annual Orange Order parade, with its associated pipe and drum bands, Orange Lodge members proudly adorned in their sashes and bowler hats and a fair sprinkling of bigots clinging desperately to an historical battle in 1690, between an Englishman and his Dutch nephew. The fact that this battle was between a Catholic ex-King James II and a Protestant King William (Billy to his friends), did much to feed the myth that the 'troubles' of Northern Ireland was a religious conflict. Then again, why let the truth get in the way of a good riot.

I do remember some acts of kindness from my Granda. He made my first tricycle from scrap parts and I helped him spray it bright blue from an aerosol can. It was my pride and joy. I even won my first race against Sandy Colligan, who had a proper Raleigh bike. No-one in Grove Street owned a car, so it became the track. The course was up Grove Street around the corner and down the alley separating Grove and Earl Streets, then completing the block back into Grove Street. We'd go so fast, we take the corners on two wheels. We became expert in remounting the bike after a spill. Arse up, head down, we'd fly around the course. But no-one flew like Sandy Colligan, with his Raleigh. Well, not until wee Johnny Wardlow arrived with his 'custom' trike. Custom sounds so much better than homemade! Sadly, like most things related to Granda, even my tricycle came to a sad end. I got a puncture in one of the tyres and reported this fact to him when he got back from work one day. I picked the wrong day. I got a swift backhander across the face and a sickening blast of alcoholic breath as he scolded,

"I made this special and you treat it like shit!"

He took the bike through the house and threw it against the end wall of the yard, breaking the frame. For weeks afterwards, tears would fill my eyes every time I went to the toilet and saw the bright blue paint slowly flaking and being defeated by rust. I was five years old.

Chapter 4 – Off to School

It was around this time that my grandparents got a break they probably deserved. It was time to send the twins off to school. The timing was excellent, as just the week before one of my father's increasingly rare visits coincided with our 5th birthday. I only have one picture of my childhood and it was taken on that day, the 30th of August 1963. Fred and I are standing face to face on the settee dressed in cowboy outfits, guns drawn. At our feet are large models of a fire engine and a locomotive.

Five years old and still losing!

If You Can't Take a Joke…

They are the only toys I remember, too. Our father's visits were always a high point, as they generally consisted of a week of days out for the whole family, with money no object. Why more of his money didn't go to my grandparents on a more regular basis to help raise his children is still a mystery to me. We'd go to the zoo or the museum and once we took a trip to the Mourne Mountains, during which I lost my cowboy gun. Thirty three years later, I went back to Ireland and found myself near the same mountains. I couldn't help but take a walk up the hills, never taking my eyes off the ground, hoping that I'd find that toy gun.

For much of my childhood, my recall is only ankle deep. Whether this is because I've suppressed a lot of bad experiences and damaging incidents or because I simply have an un-elephant-like memory, I do not know. What I do know is that I'm not at all interested in having some professional shrink have me lie down on his couch whilst he delves any deeper. I don't see how that could possibly improve my life and I fear the potential risk of re-opening well-healed wounds.

My first school was the aptly named Lancaster Street Primary School. Apt, because it was a primary school in Lancaster Street. It was a single, large Victorian brick building, with over half a century of Belfast soot providing sinister shading to the brickwork and cement. I remember that Fred and I were the youngest boys in the school, given that our birthday was at the end of August and the school year began the following week. One incident that I can recall clearly, was that on our very first day, Fred had committed the cardinal sin of speaking when the teacher was speaking. The teacher, a plump, cardigan-wrapped woman of indeterminate age, was livid at this obvious challenge to her authority. Corporal punishment was the order of the day and Fred was brought to the front of the class of around thirty children, had his trousers pulled down and was spanked until he cried. I don't remember her name, but if I did I would have printed it here in a very large font, bold, underlined and in bright red. From that day school was simply short periods of fun in the playground, interrupted by boring longer periods trying to keep warm in the chilly classroom. We learned to write with chalk on wood-framed slates and learned everything by rote, whether it be the times tables or poems by Alfred Lord Tennyson. Incredible, I know! They taught poetry at primary school.

One morning a message came to our teacher that there was to be a special assembly for all students. We all marched down to the assembly hall-cum-gymnasium and waited as a large radiogram was rolled onto the stage. The mood was curiously gloomy and even when a child made a fuss or misbehaved, there was none of the usual clips around the ear. Just a whispered,

"Tommy, shush up, there's a good lad."

Mr. Vizard, our headmaster, stepped up to the lectern and cleared his throat.

"Children, you may be aware that yesterday evening, a dreadful thing happened in America."

We looked around and caught the raised eyebrows and shrugging shoulders of our classmates. Some of the female teachers were

If You Can't Take a Joke…

dabbing at the corners of their eyes with handkerchiefs. Mr. Vizard continued,

"The President of the United States of America, John Fitzgerald Kennedy was assassinated yesterday." He paused to let the news sink in. It didn't. I don't think many of us knew what 'assassinated' meant. "We are about to hear a tribute from the BBC to President Kennedy, one of Ireland's famous sons."

The radio was switched on and a solemn BBC announcer began to speak. We tried to pay attention, but even the death of the leader of the free world has little impact on the boredom threshold of children. It started with the shuffling of feet and an increase in the throat-clearing and sniffing. The radio played part of a famous speech by JFK,

"Ask not what your country can do for you….." A child's voice rang out, "He doesn't sound very Irish to me!"

I joined the chess club, mainly because Mary Hogg was in the club and I loved her. Mary was two years ahead and possibly the most popular girl in the world. At five, my love was not based on romance, marriage, or – perish the thought, sexual want, but simply a need to be near her as often as possible. Today we'd say I misread her 'signals' when I said to her that I wanted to be her brother. That was how much I loved her. Mary, being so much more mature than me, said something like,

"I've already got five brothers and I heard my ma say to my da that she's not wanting anymore!"

I was devastated and chess was never the same afterwards.

The childhood years rolled by with the boring monotony of the Janet and John books, which taught us to read. When I was about 9-years old, even the local welfare worker realized that two oldies raising four growing kids was a bit of a challenge, so offered my grandparents a 'better' house in the next street, 102 Earl Street to be exact. As I recall, the improvement was that it had two rooms upstairs instead of our current single room. At least there would be a little more privacy, or so I thought. In the event, the house was exactly the same size and the 'improvement' was a solid partition wall cutting the one large room into two tiny ones, which actually resulted in less space for us all. As the years crawled by, the area flourished and by the time I was ten, a smattering of cars had appeared, half parked on the pavement leaving unpatriotic black tyre marks on the loyalist red, white and blue kerb stones. A red telephone box appeared on the corner and a few houses even boasted television sets. Was it merely a coincidence that the most popular kids in the street lived in those houses?

Despite these improvements, the political climate was changing. Of course, I had little interest in politics at that time, but I was conscious that the tone of the playground tittle-tattle had changed. The political leanings of the grown-ups at home were diluted by our developing minds and insults like fatty, spotty and specky-four-eyes were substituted by Fenian, Taig and Tim for the Catholics and Prod, Orangie and Jaffa for the Protestants. These monikers were usually preceded by 'dirty' and followed by 'bastard', so I was a dirty Jaffa bastard and Sean Maguire was a dirty Fenian bastard! I remembered the 12th July marches of the early 60s being all about fun and marching and bands. Every street in the loyalist areas would be festooned with flags and red-white-and-blue bunting was hung from house to house along the whole street. The kerb-stones would get a fresh coat of paint and the waste-grounds would be piled high with scrap wood for the bonfires on the evening of the 11th July to signal the start of the celebrations. It was great sport to try to pinch wood from the stockpiles of adjacent neighbourhoods, but most had overnight sentries in place to protect their bonfire. As the decade drew to a close, however, the mood had changed. Counter marches by Republican factions were organized, routes were changed and constantly surveilled by police and army patrols. The fun was disappearing.

Looking back, I guess that during those years, I was a fairly anonymous child. Skinny, much smaller than my 20-minute older twin and with fairly nondescript features. I was acutely aware that the lower my profile, the less likely I was to be picked on either by the school bullies or by my overbearing, unreasonable and unpleasant grandparents. Paul, my youngest brother, endured longer and longer stays in hospital and we used to be fascinated by each new scar that had developed whilst he was away. Back then, Paul was a midget, but today he'd have been promoted to little person, vertically challenged or spatially efficient. He didn't seem to care and would often head off in the morning with a jolly, "Hi Ho, Hi Ho, it's off to school I go!" Nonetheless, he was mercilessly teased by almost everyone. Most people accept that children can be unforgiving towards any difference and that that is perfectly normal. Let's face it, to children, people with dwarfism look funny and remind them of Snow White's little helpers. They have that funny waddle, because their legs are so short. Even better, when they get angry because you've taken the mickey, they become even funnier. Their heads are so big, it seems to amplify their facial expressions. Hilarious. Fred and I didn't find it hilarious at all. Although we were skinny little runts, there were two of us and we happily joined forces to protect our little brother. Many times, mothers of other children would arrive on our doorstep, with a crying, snotty-nosed Jimmy or Ronny, complaining to our grandparents that we had set upon their precious child. Granda, in particular, was very quick to send these women packing with a warning that there was plenty more where that came from, if Jimmy/Ronny continued to bully Paul. Then Fred and I would get a beating for making people believe that we were a family of gangsters. Sadly, Paul's trips to hospital became more frequent, with longer stays and eventually he was shipped off to Auntie Maureen's house in Portadown and we rarely saw him. We all missed him dreadfully. My grandparents had become increasingly embittered by the unfairness of being burdened by young children in what should have been their sunset years. I suppose they had a point. Granda's drinking got worse and occasionally, when his penchant for violence went too far, Granny would pile us all onto the bus to Portadown for a day or two while he calmed down. On one occasion, we returned to our house after one of these escapes, to find a note on the front door, asking us to keep the noise down as Granda was trying to sleep. Oddly, it was a very polite note in beautiful handwriting – perhaps an indication of what he might have become under different circumstances.

I fared quite well academically, but this just meant I was fair game for the bullies. Swot, teacher's pet and arse-kisser were some of the kinder insults which accompanied the pushing, shoving and school-satchel emptying at the hands of my peers. I was a sad little sod and I cried a lot. I felt small and wondered why all the big people hated me. Who was fighting for me?

Chapter 5 – Out of the Slums

There was always a lot of to-ing and fro-ing of family members during our time in Grove Street. My sister, Caroline, seemed to be taken away regularly by the social services and spent long periods in a Girl's Home.

Memories of my mother had started to fade, so when I was about ten years old I was astounded to see her in a television shop in Belfast. The surprises continued. She wasn't actually in the shop, but on about twenty television screens displayed in the shop window. Given that she had run away from a violent family environment, I suppose it was logical that she would at some point change her name. But seriously, Dusty Springfield? I was so convinced that my mother had become a successful pop star in England that I actually told anyone who asked about my parents that my father was a musician and my mother was Dusty Springfield. To be absolutely clear here, I wasn't lying. Of course, Grandma and Granda would deny it, even make a joke out of it, but deep down I knew it to be true. I soon had the opportunity to ask her to her face.

This was the year that my father completed his 22 years in the Army and was officially pensioned off. This was the year that my mother would return to the family fold after years of running. It sounds like perhaps there might be a happy ending to this miserable childhood, doesn't it? As it turned out, this was one of the most tumultuous and miserable years of my life. It sucked, it really sucked. In his last months in the Army, my father had started to make plans for the future. Despite the Royal Irish Fusiliers being an Irish regiment, they were stationed everywhere but Ireland. It was a regiment with a proud history counting the Somme, Ypres and Gallipoli in its battle roll of honour. Victoria Crosses were awarded to two of its soldiers, Private Robert Morrow and Lieutenant Geoffrey St George Shillington Cather during the First World War. As is so often the case, both men were awarded the honour posthumously.

The news that my father was to return to Belfast permanently was, as you'd expect, well received by my long-suffering grandparents. I need to make a point here about how I refer to my father. To be perfectly honest, it appears very clumsy to keep writing 'father'. It seems cold, cold, cold, especially if I try to imagine my daughters calling me that. They occasionally call me 'fazha' in a poor impersonation of Mike Myers' Austin Powers character, but I was always Daddy and then Dad, as they got older. From time to time, they will revert back to Daddy, mainly when they want something, because they know it sounds so endearing. I have considered the rather limited alternatives to father. I tried writing 'Da', which was the standard Belfast form of address and probably what I actually called him, but it doesn't sit comfortably. 'Daddy' implies affection, which was never present, and 'ass-hole' is just wrong, so 'father' it is then. Anyway, his return finally gave my grandparents the opportunity to leave behind the slums which had been their wretched lot for a lifetime for they were to move with us into our new house in Haypark Avenue in the Ormeau Road area of South Belfast. Even better, my mother had agreed to a reconciliation and was returning from England to take

If You Can't Take a Joke...

up her responsibilities as doting wife, loving mother and caring daughter. The children were to be reunited – by this time, Fred had fallen foul of the very strict legal system and was in Bawnmore Boy's Home on probation and Caroline was once again in a Girl's Home. We were to be placed in new modern schools and even have our own beds. By today's standards the house in Haypark Avenue would still be considered quite modest, but to us it was a castle. It was a terraced house, but unlike the slums of Grove Street, it had a front garden. Not much of a garden, to be fair, but the postman had to leave the street to post the mail through the door. The house had a proper hallway, with an old wooden coat hook and umbrella stand. The front room, which in Belfast in those days was imaginatively referred to as the front room or parlour, was off limits to the children and was reserved primarily for visitors. To our young slum-acclimatised eyes, the living room was massive, with a huge sofa, two arm chairs and a large television. It got better. No longer did we have to battle the cold, the rain and the shadows to go to the toilet. Upstairs was a proper indoor toilet. No, a bathroom. This house had a bathroom! Life was sweet. Our new school, Ulidia Primary School in Somerset Street, was a new building which looked bright, shiny and eager to house bright, shiny and eager kids desperate for learning. It got even better. The school was 100 yards from our front door, so no more traipsing through sleet and snow for half-an-hour to get to Lancaster Street. Things were looking up. I looked up, too. I looked up at the front door of our new house. Number 13.

Chapter 6 – From Worse to Worser

Despite the connotations of the number 13, our new house was more tragic than unlucky. Caroline, Fred, Paul, who had rejoined the family, and I had become accustomed to the disciplinarian regime of our grandparents, but our father's discipline was Army based and rigidly enforced. Over 22 years in the Army had instilled some admirable qualities in the man; punctuality, cleanliness, smartness and a yes-sir-no-sir-three-bags-full-sir obedience to both order and orders. For the guttersnipe rabble that were his children, his standards were not only high, but simply impossible for us to achieve, so punishment was bestowed almost daily. No longer the instant attitude adjustment by way of a back-hander or straightforward thrashing. Fifties and sixties kids are probably familiar with the coordination of words and strikes that seemed to encapsulate beatings of that era.

"DON'T (smack) DO (smack) THAT (smack) EVER (smack) AGAIN (smack)!"

Like our grandparents, our father had the knack of combining both the verbal and physical elements of punishment, but he had also perfected the psychological aspect. He'd make us wait. Sometimes he'd tell us when it was going to happen,

"Right, John, I've had enough of this shite. I'll see you in the front room in half an hour."

Often he'd use this time to stew and let his anger build. I'd know I was in for it, but didn't know when or what form his punishment would take. It was terrifying. At the appointed time, I'd drag my frightened, skinny carcass to the front room, where he would be waiting. His bearing was that of a Regimental Sergeant Major about to discipline an errant private. First would come the specifics of the crime, but there was never an offer to plead guilty or not guilty. Nor was there an opportunity to proffer mitigating circumstances or even a plea for clemency. His black-and-white code usually left me black-and-blue.

He was working for the Post Office now, in some sort of office job I supposed and certainly our standard of living, by the usual measures, was rising, but not the quality of our living. My mother played the role of peacemaker, but was simply no good at it. Once she tried to make a point to my father about his always jumping to conclusions and blaming Fred, in particular, for anything that went missing. Her plan was to take ten shillings out of his wallet and then when he automatically accused Fred, she would say something like,

"Actually, Darling (yeah, right!), it wasn't Fred. I took it out this morning to get my hair done. It does go to show, though, that you are a little too quick to accuse little Freddie."

Historically, my mother was never good at planning. She'd planned to leave home and become happily married. She'd planned to be a wonderful mother. She'd planned to return to Belfast, be forgiven for her earlier indiscretions and live happily ever after. Her latest plan fell at the first hurdle. Unfortunately, little Freddie and I were in the same room when my father opened his wallet and discovered the missing money, but regrettably mum was nowhere to be seen. Without a word, he lunged at Fred and grabbed him by the scruff of the neck.

Before anyone could react, he'd slapped Fred hard across the mouth and flung him against the wall. He was about to go after him again when my mother screamed,

"Stop it! It was me! I took the money!"

It was apparently just as unacceptable for my mother to take money from his wallet as it was for Fred to do so. To my horror, my father then backhanded my mother. She staggered back and her hand came to rest on a heavy glass ashtray, which she picked up and threw it hard at my father. He ducked, I didn't. I still have the scar on my forehead. Nice plan, mum.

My mother not only had her husband and kids to worry about. Her increasing bitter mother never cut her a break. Everything mum tried to do to keep the house clean and the family clothed and fed, was criticised. My grandmother always resented the attention that Granda paid to his daughter and I recall that she had once said to him, in front of the whole family,

"It's always my little girl this, my little girl that. What is going on between you two?"

The implication was clear to everyone and it was the first time that I remember an argument ending in silence and not thumps. The old lady's health, never good, rapidly deteriorated and she spent progressively more time in hospital. One day my father returned home early from the Post Office to catch Fred and I at home, having played truant from school that day. During the subsequent and perfectly routine thrashing he said,

"Here you are pissing your lives away while your Granny lies dead in hospital. Dead of a broken heart for the ungrateful little bastards she's had to raise!" Talk about breaking the news gently. No matter how hard I try, I can't imagine my grandmother having a heart to break. In those days, families were discouraged from taking children to funerals, so the day they buried my grandmother, I was in Class 7 at Ulidia Primary School.

Worse was to come for my mother only a few weeks later. In those days, no-one could afford to pay for plumbers, electricians or builders to carry out repairs or maintenance on their homes, so every man was a handyman. These were the sort of skills which had allowed my grandfather to build my tricycle five years before. When he was sober, he would let me help him with the odd jobs around the house. I felt very important passing him the screwdriver, or holding a cupboard door steady as he repaired a hinge. One morning, a drip appeared in the upstairs ceiling and from the alleyway behind the house we could see that one of the roof tiles had become dislodged. I was very keen to help my grandfather with the repairs, but was shunted off to school. When I returned, there was no-one at home. I let myself in using the key that hung from a string behind the letterbox. As usual, I made for the fridge for my after school snack, as unlike during my earlier childhood, there was always something to eat and drink in the house. This reminds me of something that my grandfather used to do back in our slum days. My grandmother always found it hard to feed a whole family on the little money that wasn't pissed away in the pub.

Sometimes my grandfather would say, "Special treat tonight, little ones. Bread and sauce. Who wants red and who wants brown?"

He always made this sound like such a treat, that we'd all get very excited, shouting out our choice of Heinz Tomato Ketchup or HP Sauce. It wasn't until many years later that my mother told me that he did this when she was a child and it only happened when there was nothing else to eat in the house. I still love HP Sauce. So, back to the kitchen. I was about to open the fridge door, when I noticed that the kitchen window was broken. I had apparently inherited my father's conclusion jumping gene and wondered what little Freddie had done this time. I went into the yard and saw the broken glass still unswept on the concrete. There was a large dark brown stain around and amongst the glass. Just then, my parents came home. I knew that something was wrong. I asked,

"Where's Granda?"

My mother took me by the hand, a bad sign, into the front room, a seriously ominous sign. She told me that while he was up on the roof, my grandfather had had a stroke and fallen. He'd been rushed to hospital, but had died. I don't remember if I cried and even now thinking back on it, I don't really feel any strong emotions. I suppose he was a good man, but his experience of two world wars, the depression, the slums, succumbing to alcohol and being lumbered late in life with a handful of kids took its toll on his personality and demeanour. He'd had a shit life, so I try to focus on the glimpses of the John Morton who made me smile. Building my bike, trying to hide the fact that we didn't have food in the house and teaching me to use a saw, screwdriver and hammer. It wasn't until many years later that I stopped seeing him as an alcoholic, but as a victim of alcoholism. And so another day of double maths, while they buried one of my grandparents.

I think my grandfather's death acted as a catalyst and accelerated some inevitable happenings. My mother was her daddy's little girl and he was her only ally in a hostile environment. The reconciliation with my father was never really going to work and, as she tried to distance herself from her overpowering husband, the distance between her children grew and her thoughts must have occasionally drifted back to her single life in swinging 60s London.

My mother disappeared. There was no dramatic parting, no sorrowful goodbyes. One day she just wasn't there anymore. I don't think my father even tried to offer an explanation. I transitioned rapidly from a withdrawn and frightened little boy to a silent, withdrawn and frightened little boy. With nobody to turn to in the event of my transgressing the Sgt. Wardlow rules, I would hide in my room and read. I would appear at meal times and eat in silence. I didn't have any friends and never went out to play. There were no after school clubs and as I was such a little runt, sport was out of the question.

We entered the 'Auntie' era. A series of women 'romanced' by my father, who would move in and try to play mummy. Some of them stayed in the spare room and some of them had extra mummy privileges and stayed in his room. They didn't stand a chance. Our house didn't do the word dysfunctional any justice at all. Fred, by this stage, was spending less and less time in school and more and more time in the shit. He'd come to the attention of the local police on numerous occasions and finally ended up in Juvenile Court. Much to the relief of my father, at aged eleven Fred was sentenced to one-to-three years in a young offenders institute called Rathgael. I missed him dreadfully and felt even more isolated and alone. By now, Caroline had been shipped off to a welfare home and Paul, who required more and more care as his stays in hospital increased in frequency, was in the care of our Auntie in Portadown. There was something positive on the horizon though. All the time I had spent alone with books in my bedroom improved my ability to learn. School was my escape from my grey and loveless home-life and I was gaining a reputation as a scholar with very good prospects. I had passed the eleven-plus and was allocated a place at Annadale Grammar School. My father would continually remind me that this was the opportunity of a lifetime and that no-one in the history of our family had ever been so lucky. In August of 1969, I was kitted out in long grey trousers and long grey socks with red hoops at the top. I could never understand why socks worn with long trousers should have anything around the top, let alone hoops. My black blazer proudly displayed the school badge on the breast pocket, a red cockatrice. I even had a school cap, which was kept well hidden from all my friends, as school caps were posh and therefore the wearer deserved a good kicking.

Chapter 7 – Round Peg, Square Hole

At this juncture, I ought to warn the eternal optimists and Oprah viewers that we will not be hearing about the young guttersnipe from the slums winning a scholarship to a posh school, earning a degree in sociology and returning in triumph to help all the other guttersnipes. Sorry. Little Johnny still has a few curve balls to avoid, sticky wickets to defend and bullets to dodge, but he's a tough little nut and he won't crack. Things will get better eventually, but not just yet. The downward slope continues for some time, but by about Chapter 12 you'll start to see some light at the end of this rather gloomy tunnel. Pessimists, on the other hand, if you are preparing for the worst, don't worry, he doesn't die at the end either. Well, he will eventually, but not during this book.

Annadale Grammar School is no more. In 1990, it was amalgamated with Carolan Grammar School for Girls and became Wellington College Belfast. Annadale was supposed to have been one of the first working-class grammar schools, but the reality was that most of the students came from middle and upper class families. Although there were scholarships for local boys who passed the eleven-plus examination, I was one of the very few poor boys there. On my first day, I remember a rather chaotic driveway as seemingly scores of shiny cars extruded scores of shiny boys. There were hoots of excitement as boys renewed their acquaintances from the previous year and a more subdued knot of smaller boys, who were like me joining the school for their first term. I made my way uneasily over to that group. I knew from the introduction booklets and information packs that were sent to me during the summer that languages were considered an important element of the curriculum at Annadale. French, German and Latin were all in the syllabus. My first linguistic challenge was, however, not in a classroom, but on that first day when I joined the nervous group of new joiners. I didn't understand what half of them were saying. They didn't have the harsh, rapid-fire and one-word-flowing-into-another burst transmissions that I had and they sounded more like those annoying English kids I'd seen on Blue Peter, with their working rockets made from old washing up bottles and elastic and their fucking Blue Peter badges. They did not add the absolutely unnecessary caveats that were common to lower class speech at the end of every sentence. Let me illustrate this by way of some examples/translations:

Posh Kids	**Wee Johnny**
That was incredibly brave.	Yer wee man's got some balls, so he has!
Good morning.	How's about ye wee man!
I am going to the cinema to watch a movie.	I'm going to the pictures to see a fillum, so I am!

I had already started to feel out of my depth, but before I could turn and run out of the school grounds, we were all herded into a massive assembly hall. We were directed to put our schoolbags up against the wall and to sit cross-legged on the floor and settle down please. The headmaster, in gowns, addressed the assembly from behind a lectern and for the first time, I heard a voice boom out with the aid of a public address system. How posh is that? Prior to this assembly I experienced only the two usual options in public addresses at primary school, namely being the back of the hall and hearing nothing or at the front being deafened and often spat upon by the lisping Mr. Visard, who became particularly fluid should there be any announcement involving shpecial shports shelections or shupervished shwimming shessions. Back at Annadale, it was,

"Welcome back, boys." and,

"An extra special welcome, of course, to our new arrivals."

The sports master informed us that a healthy body equaled a healthy mind. The matron offered assistance should that body become unhealthy and the school chaplain joked, sort of, that whilst the sports master and matron could have the body, the soul belonged to him, ha ha. The names of all the new boys were read out, followed by the house to which they had been allocated. Unlike the comprehensive schools, which simply had Form A, Form B, etc, Annadale's four houses were named after famous Irish Generals, Alexander, Dill, Montgomery and Alanbrooke. I was to be in Alexander house and off we went to our classrooms. The first week proved to be rather difficult for my father. At every opportunity, of course, he'd take great pride in telling everyone that his boy was going to Annadale. I never heard him explain that the other half of the twin set was being schooled at Her Majesty's Pleasure in the kiddy-jail that was Rathgael Training School. It seemed that every day, I'd return from school and present him with another bill. School Sports kit, winter jacket and weekly payment to the School Trip Fund all dipped significantly into the family purse. He never accepted these bills with good grace, just a warning that I'd better make sure he wasn't wasting his hard-earned cash. Occasionally, the envelope containing the bill would also reveal a letter from my form teacher complaining about my attitude or behaviour and stressing that Annadale's teachers were there to educate, not to parent its students. At home, attitude adjustment, army style, would follow.

What made my short time at Annadale all the more difficult was that none of my school pals from primary school were with me. They had all gone to Mountcollyer Secondary School and when I caught up with them at weekends, their tales of school life seemed so much more fun. One particular difference was that Mountcollyer was experimenting with giving their students no homework. No home work! The 'troubles' were well underway by now and after school clashes with the Roman Catholic students of St. Aloysius were always top of the list of adventures enjoyed by my ex-school friends. One incident that summed up my attitude, my lack of commitment and my bad luck at Annadale involved Paul Whitaker and a dart. It is also the first time I consciously recall being a 'smartass'. The evening before, at Bawnmore, one of the boys had found a dart. Darts are brill. A big, heavy brass body, bright orange flights and a very sharp point combined to provide hours of fun for a young lad. Now, although the dart was designed primarily for a game of skill, played exclusively in pubs, they could be thrown for much longer distances than the regulation 7 feet 9 inches used in the pub sport. After throwing the darts at doors, trees and anything else it would stick in, I managed to secrete it in my pocket. Just after lunch the following day, my class was suffering a double maths lesson. The United Kingdom was about to transfer our currency from the imperial pound sterling to a decimal system, so we were studying imperial to metric conversions. It will become clear why I recall the subject matter so specifically quite soon. I hated maths. I wasn't bad at it, but numbers just didn't cut it. After about 30mins of listening to the master drone on, I started to get bored. The first stage of classroom boredom usually involves simply trying not to fall asleep. Nodding off was considered quite disrespectful at Annadale and almost a cardinal sin. The second stage boredom is fidgeting. It was during this second stage that my hand dropped to my thigh and felt the outline of the dart in my pocket. I took it out and, keeping it under desk level, started fidgeting some more. Boredom Stage Three, the most dangerous, suddenly overcame me. Mischief. Paul Whitaker was sitting two rows in front of me at the extreme right of the classroom. I'm sure he was more than 7 feet 9 inches away, but I fancied my chances. A voice in my head told me that it would be hilarious if the next time the teacher turned to the blackboard to write up yet another formula, I took the dart and chucked it so that it landed in the middle of Paul's desk. The teacher turned to the board and I aimed and launched the dart. The brain is an amazing organ and even though I didn't like maths very much, I quickly realized that the trajectory of the dart was not quite right. Time slowed and I watched the flight path of the dart with increasing anxiety. Sure enough, the dart didn't quite reach the desk. To my

If You Can't Take a Joke...

horror, the dart landed in, that's in, not on, Paul's head. Initially, of course, the thought that the stinging sensation in his left temple was caused by an errant dart would have been far from his mind, but as he turned his head in my direction the bright orange flight appeared in his peripheral vision and his hand shot to his head. Upon realising that he had been impaled by a dart, he immediately screamed like a big fucking girl, prompting the master to turn back from the blackboard. By then, I had instinctively jumped to my feet and therefore had tacitly confessed. The master reached me in four paces and yelled frothily into my face,

"What makes you think you can come into my classroom an throw a dart 10 feet across the room without injuring someone?"

"I didn't."

"What?"

"I didn't try to throw it 10 feet, I tried to throw it 3.05 meters, Sir!"

"Smart ass!"

SLAP!

My ears didn't stop ringing for a week.

I began to spend less time attending school and had perfected the knack of turning up for roll call, informing my housemaster that I had a medical or dental appointment, then leave for the day and not return. Although slightly ashamed of it today, I remember once telling him that my sick brother Paul was in hospital and 'would probably not make it through the day'. Apparently on his deathbed, he had requested that his siblings be present should the worst happen. My

If You Can't Take a Joke...

schoolbag contained not a single book, but a change of clothes for my daily adventures. I also started to roam the streets until late in the evening. My father was a believer that early to bed, early to rise would make me healthy, wealthy and wise, so by eight o'clock, I would be in bed. By eight thirty, I knew he would be dozing in front of the television and would sneak downstairs, through the kitchen and out into the alley. I would meet up with the usual gathering of delinquents and we'd set off on missions of mischief. By this time, street riots were a daily occurrence and we spent many hours in the Markets area of south Belfast. We were too young to be proper members of the Loyalist paramilitaries, but we would definitely join once we left school. In the meantime, being fairly small as well as young, we couldn't join in the proper riots either. What we did, was to station ourselves behind the ranks of soldiers with their helmets, tear gas and rubber bullet guns and throw stones and bricks over their heads to the rioting Catholic youths in front of them. The soldiers, focused on avoiding petrol bombs and rocks coming from ahead, would ignore us until eventually one of our bricks would fall short and clatter against a helmet, one of, head protecting for the use of. We were too young for them to 'fight', so one of them would turn around and chuck a tear gas bomb at us and we'd scarper back towards our home turf. Sometimes I'd arrive home as late as three o'clock in the morning, sneak in through the kitchen window and then be up at seven for breakfast and school. Ah, the good old days.

Chapter 8 – The Great Escape

Playing truant was much more fun than going to school, so eventually I stopped going at all. I didn't think anyone cared anyway, but looking back, I didn't really give anyone the opportunity to care. The school clearly thought that I was a sickly child and my father thought I was in regular attendance at Annadale. In those days, the postman delivered the mail at around eight o'clock in the morning and it was my daily mission to ensure that I was in the hallway before the letterbox flap had stopped swinging. At the six week mark, I'd successfully intercepted about a dozen envelopes with the Annadale Grammar School cockatrice proudly embossed on the top left hand corner of the letter. After about the third letter, I began to wonder how long my luck would hold. The theme of the correspondence was always the same, but the tone became increasingly prickly and the more prickly they became, the more tangled became the web I was weaving. Not only was I not going to school, I was stealing. Every Monday morning, my father would give me an envelope to take to school. It contained my bus fare, lunch money and also the weekly payment to the School Trip Fund. No internet transfers, credit cards or cheques back then, just cold hard cash. I was loaded! I'd hate you to think that I was having an easy life during that period of prolonged absence from school. Far from it. These days I'm still surprised that on any given school day, I can visit a shopping mall and see lots of school aged kids hanging around the food court or outside the music store. No one cares. In Belfast in the early 1970s, a child couldn't get

If You Can't Take a Joke...

100 yards, without a school truant officer, policeman or cantankerous old busy-body asking why he wasn't at school. Both police and truant officers had the power to detain you until they were satisfied that non-attendance was legitimate. Not only that, the streets were heavily patrolled by mobile army squads, known colloquially as snatch squads. Given that every night they were enduring a lot of abuse and projectiles from the youth of Belfast, they were also happy to sweep unaccompanied youngsters of the street. It also meant that they'd have to take them back to the barracks to have their stories confirmed and this meant a hot cup of tea and a biscuit for them. All this meant that each day had to be planned with surgical precision. Food supplies for the day had to be procured before school started, items to ward of boredom were sourced and, most importantly, a safe haven had to be found. With cash in my pocket and no adult guidance, food consisted of a foot-long fresh cream filled bun from the bakery and pockets full of sweets from the corner shop – blackjacks, sherbet flying saucers, pear drops and Caramac bars. To keep myself occupied, I always ensured that I had something to read. By this time I'd outgrown the Beano, Dandy, Beezer and Topper and had moved onto the Hotspur and Wizard and, if I was lucky, copies of MAD magazine were available. The biggest daily challenge was finding a hide-out and this was very much weather dependent. On dry days, the Ormeau Park was a great place to spend the day. It was a large park and well-wooded, so provided plenty of opportunity to settle down in the undergrowth for a lazy day of reading and gorging on sweets. Army and police patrols didn't bother coming into the park, but from time

to time the park keeper could be spotted picking up litter or haranguing his gardeners, as they mowed grass, trimmed shrubbery or, more often than not, stood around smoking and leaning on their rakes, spades and forks. Inclement and cold weather brought different challenges.

Eventually my luck ran out. I came home one day, having changed back into my school uniform. As I reached through the letterbox to snatch the key, the door opened. My father simply said,

"Front room."

I dropped my satchel on the lino'd floor of the hallway and entered the parlour. To my horror, surprise and utter, utter disbelief right there on one of the comfy chairs sat my housemaster, dunking a Rich Tea biscuit into a cup of steaming tea. He popped the soggy end of the biscuit into his mouth, balanced the remainder on the saucer and took a moment to savour and swallow the biscuit. He said,

"Hello there, stranger."

I can't remember his name, which isn't surprising given that I hadn't spent much time in his company, but I do recall that there was nothing malicious or malevolent in his greeting. My father took his place on the other comfy chair and motioned me to sit on the settee. As I sat, I offered up a silent prayer that the settee would swallow me up whole. I looked at my father, waiting for him to begin speaking, but the teacher cleared his throat and I turned to him. I can't remember exactly what he said, but I know that the longer he spoke, the better I began to feel. He was extremely understanding about the difficulties of a boy with my background attending Annadale. He understood that sometimes running away from problems might seem like a good idea. He presented a proposal, what today would probably be called an Action Plan, which would allow me to return to school, work for an hour a day after school in the library to help me pay of my debts and put all this nonsense behind me. He told me that he'd had a long chat with my father, who was in agreement with the proposal. I felt the beginnings of relief, which would soon develop into elation, having 'gotten away with it', but one glance at my father and I immediately suppressed those feelings. After some more "my door is always open" encouragement from my housemaster he rose to leave.

"Great to have you back, Johnny," he said ruffling my hair as he left.

I'd followed them out into the hallway and as the door closed behind my teacher, my father simply said,

"Kitchen."

I picked up my satchel and saw that the kitchen door to the yard was open and, as it was about six o'clock on a winter's day in Belfast, it was already getting dark. My father guided me with a hand in my back through the kitchen door and into the cold concrete yard.

"Take off that uniform, you are disgracing it," he ordered.

I dropped the bag and slowly removed the jacket, jumper shirt and tie and folded them carefully into a laundry basket beside the clothes line. I stood there shivering in my trousers and vest.

"All of it," he growled.

Shoes and socks, followed by carefully folded trousers joined the rest of my uniform, leaving me in my vest and underpants.

"Everything."

I started to cry and felt very angry at myself for doing so, because I didn't feel like a child. My father repeated,

"Everything!"

As I removed my underwear, he uncoiled the garden hose,

"You came into this world with nothing and that is exactly what you deserve."

With those words, he turned the freezing water on me. He hosed me until every part of my body was shivering and continued to hose me as my legs gave way and I fell onto the floor of the yard. He hosed me as I curled into the foetal position trying to cover up the shame.

Finally, the hose was turned off and, in army fashion, was coiled correctly and stowed neatly on its holder. He stepped across me and into the kitchen, saying,

"You stay there and think about all the shit you've put me through. This isn't over."

He slammed the kitchen door behind him, leaving me in the yard. You know what, it was fucking over. I don't really know what came over me, but I felt a resolve I'd never known before. Perhaps the weeks of fending for myself during my lengthy truancy had given me a level of independence and confidence I never knew I could possess. Maybe I was just angry. I got up and quickly dried myself off as best I could with my school uniform, dropping it into the puddles of freezing water when I finished. I still had my street clothes in my satchel and hopping around trying to get warm, I dressed. I stood there for a moment, considering a final act of defiance, but in the end, I simply went through the gate into the alley and left Haypark Avenue, number 13, for good.

Chapter 9 – The 'Outside'

Once I had made my decision to leave, I felt a huge surge of confidence and a huge weight lift from my shoulders. I knew I was doing the right thing and I knew more than anything that I would never go back. It was a cold and wet evening, even without the garden hose, and I was ill prepared. I needed some warm clothes, as all my satchel had contained was a pair of jeans, a shirt and a pair of trainers. I was still chilled to the bone from my hosing and even walking as briskly as I was able, wasn't warming me up. Instead of walking down the streets, I stuck to the alleyways jumping up in the hope of seeing a washing line full of clothes. Of course, it quickly dawned on me that no-one would be daft enough to put clothes out to dry in this weather. I lucked upon a nightwatchman outside a building site, warming himself beside a warm brazier – a rusty oil drum with holes punched in the sides and topped up with coal. I approached cautiously, but he was friendly enough and told me to come closer and get myself warmed up. Nightwatchmen were generally retired dockers or council workers looking to top up their pensions with a few hours cash-in-hand work. He could see that I was suffering and poured me a cup of hot, sweet tea from his flask, as I explained to him that my dad was delayed at work and I didn't have a key. He obviously didn't buy my story, but didn't pry. We sat quietly, the only noises being the occasional pop of coal or hiss of steam as rain hit the sides of the brazier during short showers. Soon, I would have to move on. One of the problems with rain was that it stopped most outdoors activity, including the riots. This meant that the army patrols weren't occupied in defending themselves from bricks, bullets and bombs, so there was a noticeable increase in the number of mobile patrols. Eventually, one of them would stop and ask what I was doing. I needed to get under shelter, but not before finding some warmer clothes. Despite my earlier assertion to myself that I'd never go back to Haypark Avenue, it was the only place where I knew I could guarantee warm clothing would be available. Cursing my impetuousness, I set off. I did not want to get caught by my father, as he told me that the treatment doled out to me earlier was not the end. I tried to work out what his reaction would have been, when he returned to the yard to find me gone and my school uniform trampled into the dirty puddles. I didn't want to make any noise when I left, so I hadn't closed the door to the alley. I imagined that he'd have dashed through the door in the hope of seeing me scampering away, but by then I was long gone. He might have reported my absconding to the police, but they didn't have the assets to search for missing children. There was only one way to find out and that was to go home and see. Sticking to the alleyways again, I found myself outside the back door of number 13. Although the house was dark, I could only see the rooms at the back of the house, so it was possible that my father was in the front room, either awaiting my return or a visit from the police. I gently pushed the gate and found it securely locked. I looked up at the top of the wall, trying to figure out a way passed the shards of broken bottles along the top. I reckoned that if I could find some scrap cardboard, I could drape it across the glass, but first I had to go around the block to the front of

If You Can't Take a Joke…

the house to make sure that all the lights were off. I had to duck behind a garden wall in Haypark Avenue as I heard the approach of a mobile army patrol. Luckily they were in a vehicle. It was probably too late, too cold and too wet to be defending the nation on foot. From the other side of the road, the house was totally black. Brilliant. I was about to head back to the alley, when I remembered the key behind the letterbox. I knew our front gate squealed like a stuck pig when opened, as since my grandfather died no-one had bothered to oil the hinges, so I hopped over the low wall. Gingerly, I slid my fingers into the slot and located the string and pulled out the key. I inserted it into the lock and inch by inch pushed the door open. I was very familiar with moving stealthily around the house in the dark, because of my previous nocturnal adventures in the Markets. I knew every squeaky stair and floorboard. I got to the bedroom and closed the door quietly behind me. I didn't have much stuff and didn't even own a bag. I just started putting clothes on over the top of those I was wearing. I pulled a pillowcase off my pillow and stuffed it with socks, pants and a towel. I looked around at my posters, my one-shelf with a few books and old ashtray with my small collection of coins that my father had brought back from his travels. I didn't need anything else. I had a pillowcase and the clothes, albeit more than the required amount, on my back. I was good.

The return trip to the front door was uneventful and soon I was in the hall. As I passed the coat and umbrella stand, I saw my father's keys, loose change and wallet sitting in their usual position. I didn't hesitate. I swept up his possessions and then I was quickly back on the street. I toyed with the idea of breaking a window, or knocking the door and telling my father to fuck off, but instead, I took the cash from his wallet, pocketed the change and dropped his wallet and keys into the nearest drain. I turned my back on him and that house. To my good fortune, he wasn't alone in the house that night. His latest 'Auntie' was a short, square and unpleasant woman called Rita. She was one of the lucky ones though, because during her tour-of-duty, I was the only child in the house. We didn't get along and simply ignored each other. The reason why her presence in number 13 was to my advantage was that I knew where her house was. Her home was a council house, but she hadn't given it up when she moved in with us, just in case things didn't work out with my father. It wasn't too far to her house and now much better prepared for the weather, I set off and for the first time in my life I understood the expression 'a spring in his step'. When I arrived at Rita's house, the back alley was my first stop. I managed to use the packed pillowcase as a buffer between me and the broken glass atop the wall. I had so many layers of clothes on at this point, the pillowcase was probably redundant anyway. It did come in useful, though, as padding for my fist as I shattered a small square pane in the kitchen window. Reaching up inside, I undid the latch and I was in. My main concern now was to ensure that occupation couldn't be recognized from the front street, so I restricted myself to the rear of the house. Rita had been on Auntie duty for a while, so the fridge was empty and switched off, but there were some dry goods still left in the larder. A packet of rice, some tinned beans and vegetables and, happy days, some boiled sweets were amongst the comestibles.

These days, I fancy myself as an amateur chef, but I can tell you now that nothing I've tasted since was more satisfying than the tin of beans that I greedily wolfed down that night. Later as I lay in Rita's bed, warmed and embraced by a thick quilt, I knew that what I was doing was wrong. Running away from home, stealing money and breaking into someone's house were all actions, which could see me in serious trouble. I was too happy to care. I was warm, I had food in my belly and I was free of 13 Haypark Avenue, the ghosts of my grandparents, the memories of my mother and, most importantly, the tyranny of my father. My teacher had left our house at around six o'clock that evening and it can't have been later than midnight by the time I fell asleep. Six hours consisting of drama, violence, cruelty, realization and flight. Possibly the best six hours of my life.

    I awoke early next morning, excited but with some feelings of trepidation. In my head, I went over the events of the previous evening and felt no feelings of guilt or doubt. My resolve was intact. I made sure that the back door and gate were unlocked, so that should Rita unexpectedly return, I had my escape route prepared. I hunted around the kitchen and found some tea leaves, put the kettle on and had my first cup of black tea. My young and unrefined palate didn't enjoy the experience at all. It was time to go shopping. I was still pre-dawn and the only sound in the street was the electric hum of a milk float. The rattle of crates of milk and squeal of brakes as the milkman stop-started his way down the road gave me an idea. I threw on my coat and left the house through the back gate. I made my around to the street and checked the doorsteps of the neighbouring houses. Not only did the milky deliver milk, he also dropped off bread, eggs and cheese to his customers. Within minutes, I was back in the house with a cup of hot, sweet and milky tea and tucking into scrambled eggs on toast. This became my routine for a week or so. I was afraid to venture outside the house during the day in case a nosy neighbour spotted me. I knew that eventually I'd have to leave this house, but had no plan as to where to go from there. During the day, the house continued to provide useful treasures. Rita was a smoker and collected the coupons from every pack. These could be redeemed for toasters, kettles and other domestic essentials from the Embassy Catalogue, but more importantly could be sold in the local shops. Green Shield Stamps, a loyalty reward from various shops and garages were the same and Rita, bless her, was an avid collector. After a few days, I decided that I couldn't simply spend my life in this house. I started to venture out regularly and started to meet other kids of my age, who were also social outcasts. I remember one individual in particular. He was called Tab Hunter. He was the coolest person I'd ever met. Tall, slim and handsome, he had the air of the rebel about him. Shit, just look at his name – Tab Hunter! He was a couple of years older than me and the street had been his home for some time. He wore an old army greatcoat and Dr. Marten boots and had street cred oozing out of every pore. He was a magnet to all the younger kids, as he leaned against a wall with a cigarette dangling from the corner of his mouth, which was just about as cool as you could get. He took me under his wing and began to educate me in the skills required to survive my new lifestyle. He was an intelligent boy, never missing an opportunity to stick his nose into a book and possessed a knack with words that both impressed and amused me. We were not homeless, or urchins running around stealing and shoplifting, but 'living on the outside, liberating survival essentials'. He made me a 'junior partner' in his 'enterprise', by teaching me how to act as decoy, while he stuffed food into bags sewn into the inside of his greatcoat. He showed me a number of decoy strategies, including simply looking suspicious, misbehaving just enough to be thrown out of the store and, my favourite, removing a can from a pyramid display resulting in scores of tins of beans toppling and rolling down the aisles. While I had the attention of the security guard, there was only ever one on duty in those days, Tab would be busily filling his bags. He taught me to target small and expensive items, rather than bulky goods. We went for cheese, coffee, toiletries and cosmetics. Tab knew all the local characters, including those who were prepared to buy stolen goods from us. We stayed in derelict houses, of which there were many, but never for more than a couple of days before moving on. I got to know all the nightwatchmen in the area, as on particularly cold nights, their glowing braziers were the only source of warmth. Of course, we never did any laundry and based our cleanliness regime on our sense of smell. When it was determined that one or other of us began to 'hum' too much, we go clothes shopping from the local washing lines. I would simply go for the clothes line which had anything which looked like it might fit. Tab, on the other hand, had his image to consider and we'd spend hours trying to find just the right jeans and shirts. It was around this time that I also started to smoke, as I reckoned it was time that I upped my reading on the coolness scale. Players' Number Six was the cheapest brand, or if you were very brave, you'd go for unfiltered Park Drive, which rumour had it were made from the floor sweepings of the Gallaher's cigarette factory. This started my lifelong addiction to nicotine, but sadly did nothing for my cool factor. I was a skinny, mop-haired, pug-nosed little runt and it was going to take more than a cigarette to make me cool. As the weeks passed, I became accustomed to my new life, but it was obvious even to me, that it couldn't last forever.

Chapter 10 – The System

As well as truant officers, police officers and army squads, social workers also regularly patrolled the streets. These were generally young university graduates with a social conscience, who genuinely wanted to help the disadvantaged. They were not like the police, in that they didn't insist that you went with them for processing. Often, they would find us around the braziers and just come to chat. With the dull orange glow of the fire reflected in our faces, they tried to adopt street-speak and would indulge our bad habits,

"How about a fag, kid?"

Even if they didn't smoke, they would always carry a packet of Number Sixes, so that they could bond. To be fair, they had the best of intentions, they didn't hassle us and they cared. It was one of these social workers that eventually persuaded me to get off the streets. I wish I could recall his name, but like so many things, it has become lost in the clutter of other memories from that time. As you'd expect, his priority was to get me to return home, as this would prove less of a burden on the social security budget than having me in a welfare home. I was never pressured to give my full name, but I suspected he knew who I was simply by checking the police list of runaways.

"Johnny, tell me who your dad is and I'll go talk to him, you know, mend some fences. I'm sure he's worried about you."

"Johnny, imagine being back home tonight in a warm bed, instead of dossing down out here."

Bless his little cotton socks, he had no idea what it was like to live in 13 Haypark Avenue. He was always very kind to me and would often drop his loose change into my hand as he left to seek out other runaways. One particularly miserable night, as I stood rubbing my hands together beside the brazier unable to get rid of the chilled to the bone feeling after a day of wandering aimlessly around in that fine Belfast drizzle, that same social worker found me. Recognising, I suppose, that my resolve was being bent by the want of a proper meal and warmth, he invited me back to one of the welfare facilities, which doled out hot Irish stew and bread rolls to homeless adults. He put me at a corner table well away from the long-term drop-outs, druggies and divvies and fetched me a steaming bowl of lamb and vegetables smothered in a rich brown gravy. I felt its warmth go deep into my body and radiate outwards, slowly removing the chill from my bones.

"Johnny, it's been a while now, so why don't you let me take you home, eh? I'll drive you myself, so I will."

I could sense that he was genuinely trying to help me, so I told him why he couldn't. I cried again as I told him of my grandparents, my sister and brothers and the cruelty of my father. I could see the compassion and pity turning to anger. He sat thoughtfully for a few minutes and then I could see that he had come to a decision.

"Right, Johnny, you're coming with me and don't worry, you won't have to go home. I've got room in my house for the night and tomorrow morning, I'll find you somewhere permanent."

I remembered Tab Hunter warning me that there were some men, who found homeless boys and took them back to their houses, or

If You Can't Take a Joke...

somewhere, and fiddled with them, but somehow I knew this man was not one of those. I had just warmed up and the thought of drifting around the cold, damp streets looking for somewhere to sleep frightened me for the first time. I accepted his offer.

The next morning we set off for the offices of the social services. Over breakfast, the social worker – God, I wish I could remember his name – explained that there was nothing to worry about. He would just ring around and see if any of the homes had room for one more boy. Bawnmore Boys Home, right beside the new M2 motorway had a vacancy. Rather like posh public schools, I believe they let me in because my brother Fred was an 'old boy'. My friend, the social worker, took me to Bawnmore personally and as we drove up the long drive off Mill Road, he said,

"It'll take some getting used to, but give it a chance, Johnny. Give it a chance, for me?"

I told him I would do my best. He presented me to a member of staff and headed back down the drive. I never saw him again, but although I've forgotten his name, I'll never forget his compassion and kindness.

Bawnmore Boys Home was a council run welfare home in the Greencastle area on the outskirts of Belfast and like so many of the locations of my childhood, it no longer exists. It housed around 25 boys who, for one reason or another, did not have a proper home. The Home was managed by Mr. Smith, a middle-aged, graying and slightly overweight man, who didn't quite acquire 'jolly' status, but was close. He did not appear to have much to do with the day-to-day running of the house, but unlike some previous authority figures, his arrival in the dining room or dormitory wasn't greeted with feelings of uncertainty or foreboding. The house itself was a hefty, rambling Victorian affair, with a large hallway and wide staircase leading to the dormitories upstairs. Compared to Grove Street and even Haypark Avenue, it was massive. There were cupboards under the stairway that were bigger than the bedrooms in Grove and Earl Streets and the dormitories had about eight beds in each. It had large bathrooms and even its own laundry. The grounds were enormous and for those of us whose only real exposure to space was the waste grounds near our homes, it was like living in the country. We weren't locked in and the only fences were to protect the boys from the newly commissioned M2 motorway, which ran just to the south of the house and grounds. The staff consisted of young social workers, young enough not to have become cynical or disillusioned, so we were looked after very well. The only difficulties were generally created by the boys themselves. For the first time, I started to become aware of the 'code'. The code is the unwritten rules of any establishment, developed by the members or inmates, in order to ensure that the authorities were kept in the dark about any infractions of the normal rules. Revealing confidential information or squealing to staff was unacceptable and was generally rewarded by a 'good kick in the bollicks'. The official responsibilities of Bawnmore like keeping the boys warm, fed and sheltered fell squarely on the shoulders of the staff, but general behavior was policed by the older boys. I remember one boy in particular, Jim Rankin, who was not only the oldest boy, but the toughest. He was

If You Can't Take a Joke...

the King of Bawnmore. He used to make the younger boys massage his feet every night until he fell asleep. He also organized, and this may not surprise you, wanking competitions with the winner being the first to 'shoot his load'. I never felt more insignificant as when I watched the older boys grabbing fistfuls of engorged man-meat, as I frantically rubbed my peanut twixt thumb and forefinger. I never won. We were at an age at which sexual matters became increasingly prominent. There was one boy, let's call him Gerald, who attended the 'special' school. He was a sad, lonely lad with a four-year-old mind directing a 15-year-old body, penis included. It was well known to us other boys, that we shouldn't find ourselves alone with Gerald, but it was never quite clear why. I found out the hard way. There was a densely wooded area in the grounds of the home and one day I heard Gerald call my name from the edge of the trees.

"Johnny, Johnny, I've made a camp. Come and see!"

He disappeared into the woods and I followed. I found him in a small clearing. I looked around and although I could not see a tent, I couldn't miss the pole. Gerald grabbed me by the scruff of the neck with one hand and his giant penis with the other.

"Suck it," he demanded, pushing my head towards the monster.

I had no idea why he'd want me to do such a thing and I didn't want to find out. My hands were free and as hard as I could, I punched him in the balls. He released his hold on my neck and I scarpered. Of course, the code would not allow me to report the incident to the staff, but I never allowed myself within ten feet of Gerard ever again.

If You Can't Take a Joke...

There were only boys at Bawnmore and Dunlambert, my new school, was a boys only school, so our firsthand knowledge of girls was minimal. We did not have internet or girly magazines and sex education was an absolute no-no in Northern Ireland at that time. We also didn't have fathers, so we also didn't get the 'chat', which was probably more dreaded by the fathers than the sons. So we were in the dark. You may find it incredulous that young teenage boys were so naive, given that the sexual revolution was well underway just across the water in England, but back then Belfast, although catching up, was culturally years behind the UK mainland. I think I may have been the first of our group to see a naked woman. One of the staff was Miss Mary, in her early 20s and probably an undergraduate getting work experience between semesters at university. She was kind and gentle, but most importantly to the boys she was fucking gorgeous. Every night, as his feet were being massaged by some unlucky little runt, Rankin would let everyone know exactly what he'd like to do to Miss Mary. I didn't know what he was talking about half the time, but it definitely sounded like he had plans to put things where they didn't belong. The staff had a duty roster and would sleep in the house on their day of duty, so that they could get the boys up in time for breakfast and school, or whatever activity was planned during the holidays. During my time at Bawnmore, I became a fairly frequent bed-wetter and those of you who have suffered this condition, will know the shame and embarrassment of telling your mother about your 'accident'. What I used to do was very quietly get up before very everyone else, take off the bedsheets and put them in the laundry and then sneak into the staff bathroom to steal a fresh set from the huge linen cupboard. I didn't care that the mattress was still wet. The discomfort of slowly freezing in a damp bed the following night was nothing compared to the shame and embarrassment of admission. One morning, I had successfully stripped the bed, sneaked out of the dorm, down the corridor and shoved the wet sheets through the hatch into the laundry room. I followed my usual routine and stealthily set off for the staff bathroom. I gently turned the doorknob and pushed on the door. It was stuck and didn't budge. Keeping as quiet as possible, I push harder. Nothing. I had to get fresh sheets as the beds were always checked to see if they had been made properly and without sheets, it would be obvious that something was amiss and my soggy mattress would be discovered. I was becoming desperate, so I put my shoulder to the door and pushed hard. The door gave way and as I stumbled into the bathroom, just as Miss Mary was standing up to get out of her bath. We both froze. The bath was slightly raised and I was only a little chap, so my eyes were exactly level with, and only about a foot away from, her 'privates'. I say privates, because this was the only word I knew at the time. Finally, she screamed,

"Get out, get out!"

I explained that I only wanted to get some sheets, but it appeared that she did not really want to continue our conversation,

"GET OUT NOW!"

Her screams had drawn the attention of another staff member, who bounded up the stairs just in time to see me flying out of the bathroom, propelled by a slamming door to the arse. After breakfast,

I was summoned to Mr. Smith's office. He explained that he knew what happened in the staff bathroom and understood that it was all an accident. Of course, he'd also found out that I'd wet the bed, which was far more embarrassing to me. He asked me not to mention the incident to the other boys and suggested,

"We'll just put it all behind us."

Don't mention it to the other boys? The single most exciting thing that had ever happened to me and don't mention it to the other boys? I don't think so. That night after lights out, the boys all wanted to know why I had been sent for by Mr. Smith. I told them the whole story, leaving out the reason why I went to the staff bathroom, of course. There was a deathly hush as I drew out the description of a naked Miss Mary, right down to the triangle of hair around her privates, which drew a couple of groans from under jerking sheets. Just as the admiration of the boys was complete, Jim Rankin said cruelly,

"You lying little fucker, I heard you pissed the bed!"

Bastard.

Schooling was taken care of by the local schools and, having burned my bridges with Annadale, I was sent off to Dunlambert Secondary School. I recall nothing of my time there, as I had fortunately arrived just days before the Easter Holidays of 1971, so barely had time to etch my name into my desk with a compass before the long Easter break. During that break, I had my first meeting with my new social worker, Brian. Brian was strange. He used to take me and a couple of the other boys for a drive in his car. He'd drive to the M2 and then allowed us to take it in turn to sit on his lap and drive the car. This seemed to make him happy and on the way back he'd buy us an ice-cream.

"Did you enjoy driving the car, boys?"

We'd nod, our mouths too full of Mr. Whippy (relax, it is an ice cream) to reply.

"Well, make sure you don't tell the staff. It's against the law for boys to drive and you wouldn't want to get me into trouble now, would you?"

Things that make you go,

"Hmmm".

We'd occasionally have meetings with Mr. Smith to see how we were getting along. At one such meeting, he asked me what I'd like better than anything in the world. I told him that I missed my brother, Fred, and that I'd like to be with him.

"Ah, Johnny, Fred's in Rathgael and only bad boys go to Rathgael."

I took this as advice, but probably not in the way that Mr. Smith intended.

Chapter 11 – 'Outside' Again

I was actually quite a good boy. I didn't steal as much as others, I was only as disrespectful to the staff as was required to avoid being labeled a crawler and most of my rebellious activities were driven by unhappy circumstance rather than malice. However, Mr. Smith had clearly said,

"Only bad boys go to Rathgael."

I gave them bad. I knew that two other boys, Dusty Rhodes and Ronnie Wilson, weren't particularly happy at Bawnmore and together we planned our escape. Escape may be a little dramatic, as I've pointed out previously we weren't locked in the home at any stage. All we had to do was walk down the lane. Given that the population of Bawnmore Boys Home consisted of troubled youth, incidents of boys walking down the lane and not coming back were not uncommon. The usual routine on discovery of a missing boy, usually at meal times, was for the staff to jump in their cars and do a local search. Often boys just forgot the time and were late, rather than missing. If this initial search proved fruitless, the police would be informed, details taken and local bobbies briefed. The army was also informed and, more than once, a boy would be returned by one of the infamous 'snatch squads'. We left the home early one afternoon straight after lunch. This would give us the maximum getaway time, before our mission would be discovered. The objective was to get as far away as possible from Bawnmore, which would reduce our chances of being spotted by the local Constabulary who were familiar with all three of

If You Can't Take a Joke...

us. I don't think that Dusty or Ronnie had ulterior motives for absconding, but were simply excited to be going on an adventure. Riots and bombings were now as much a part of Belfast daily life as potato-bread and we had to avoid the Catholic areas, at all costs. Gangs of teenage IRA-wannabees and future UDA-candidates would patrol the streets in their combat jackets and balaclavas and carry out spot-checks on strangers on their patch. If you were of the wrong denomination, nothing could protect you from a severe beating. I had been stopped on a number of occasions during my time with Tab Hunter, but regardless of which side stopped me, I'd always pass safely through. This was because Tab had taught me the words to The Sash, a protestant anthem celebrating the Orange Order and also how to say the Hail Mary, the Roman Catholic prayer, as these were the primary test questions of the balaclava wearing hoodlums.

Dusty, Ronnie and I made our way to the Shankill Road area of Belfast. This was the hotbed of Loyalist fervour and bigotry. It was a no-go area for Roman Catholics and, for long periods during the troubles, the army as well. The whole area showed signs of a city on the verge of civil war. Many of the streets were blockaded with burnt out buses and littered with glass, bricks and other detritus left over from the most recent riot. The smell of burning rubber lingered permanently in the air, as burning car tyres was a popular addition to the blockades. We met up with an-ex Bawnmore boy, whose parents had no problem harbouring runaways, not because of a deep understanding of disturbed youths, but simply because they didn't give a shit. The ironically named 'peace wall', a thirty foot high construction designed to keep the warring factions apart, ran down the middle of the street and we'd lie in the doorway watching tracer bullets and the occasional blast bomb fly over the wall. So it was, back on the 'outside' again. As with any adventure, the first few days were exciting and the high risk environment that was Belfast in those days only fed our self-image as outlaws and rebels. When we were together, we were an invincible band of brothers, but as the days drew on, we'd spend increasing periods apart. Dusty and Ronnie would go off to their home turf for a couple of days at a time, no doubt to be hero-worshipped by their local acquaintances. It was during these periods that a growing awareness of how lonely and pointless my existence was came over me. I hadn't absconded from Bawnmore to be a street urchin. I had a plan and it was time to put that plan into action. When Dusty and Ronnie had returned from one of their expeditions, I convinced them that life would be so much easier if we had money and that the only way to get money was burglary. We couldn't go to the middle-class areas, as we'd stick out like sore thumbs, so we stayed in the lowly Shankhill Road area. One of my major concerns was to ensure that I got caught. Now although my plan had to result in capture at some point, I had to be very careful about who was to catch me. This was an era when the Shankill and Falls Roads were policed by the UDA and IRA respectively. This was not because of any socially minded desire for justice, but to ensure that the local population knew who was in charge. Both the UDA and IRA had pseudo-military structures, including Battalions, Regiments and Squads and ruled their territories with violent rhetoric and iron fists. They would hastily convene Kangaroo courts to deal summarily with offences ranging from theft, drug dealing, providing information to the army or police and, of concern to me, burglary. There were no lawyers, no police and no appeals process. Justice was swift and ranged from a good kicking for minor offences, tarring and feathering to 'send a message' to everyone else, to knee-capping, the removal of the knees by shooting or even by drilling. In 1972, my own Uncle Tommy became a victim and was murdered by the Ulster Volunteer Force. Tommy Wardlow was a 34-year-old family man, with no connections to paramilitaries and no criminal record. He was shot from a passing car for the crime of being a Roman Catholic.

My Plan A was to get caught during a burglary by the owner of the property, who would then call the police and I'd be off to court and Rathgael, with the UDA none the wiser. There was no Plan B. What I had to avoid, at all costs, was for my appearance in court to result in a slap on the wrist and returned to Bawnmore. That meant that my offences had to be serious enough for me to be incarcerated and this meant I had to be a serial offender. I estimated that six or so burglaries would get me in deep enough poo to ensure a custodial sentence. So I set about making some of the local residents, who were already poor and could least afford it, a little poorer.

Chapter 12 – Don't Try This At Home

If you are an adrenaline junkie and have already skydived, bungee-jumped and hiked the Inca Trail, I've got a suggestion for your next 'high'. Try being in someone else's house, without their permission, stealing their stuff. For an added burst of adrenaline, ensure that the house is in a combat zone with more than one militia keen to catch you in the act. I've done a lot of things in my time and some I've done very well. Burglary was not one of them. Of the three of us, I was the most incompetent – by far. The boys could scale a yard wall, glass topped, with the agility of a gibbon, whilst I had to wait in the alley for them to open the back gate from inside. Whereas Ronnie or Dusty could break a kitchen window using a rolled up jacket to stifle the noise, leaving only the faintest tinkle of glass heard falling into the sink, I'd try the same technique only to have a giant pane of glass fall outwards and land on the concrete yard with a sound reminiscent of small explosion in a cymbal factory. Inside the house, we were only interested in cash - a rare find, cigarette coupons or Green Shield Stamps or, the Holy Grail, the gas meter. There were no gas bills in the poorer parts of Belfast, as the gas companies realized that there would be little chance of them ever being settled, so gas was brought into the home by way of a coin-operated meter. The meters were built tough, so as to discourage the residents from helping themselves to a gas company discount during tough times. Of course they were easy meat for burglars, who didn't care about disguising the fact the meter had been tampered with, so Ronnie and Dusty made short work of them. Given my previous demonstrations of poor burgling skills, I was not allowed near the meters for fear of dislodging them entirely and filling the house with gas. Now, I'd read enough crime thrillers to have just enough knowledge to make me dangerous. I knew, for example, that in order for the police to realize that they had a serial offender on their hands, they'd profile crime scenes to determine the perp's M.O. and identify his 'signature'. My signature was to put the plug in the kitchen sink drain and leave the tap running. I know - what an asshole. Within a couple of weeks, we'd done enough burglaries for me to arrange for the capture of 'Waterboy', 'Aqua-Thief' or whatever name the police now knew me by. We were just about finished at the next house and as we were leaving I said to the boys,

"Go on ahead. I'm just going to check upstairs again. I'll see you back at the house."

I put the plug in the drain, turned on the water and sat down and waited. It was late afternoon and as it got darker, so did my imagination. I don't think I wanted to face the reality of an old lady coming home and finding a little shit like me in her flooded house and maybe dropping dead of a heart attack on the spot. I didn't want a couple of latchkey kids coming home from school either. I needn't have worried. I heard the grate of a key being inserted in the front door and stood up. The door stood open and the doorway and the entrance was filled not by a little old lady or school kids, but by a very, very large man. I rapidly determined that Plan A might be flawed and turned to run out the back door. Unfortunately, by now there was a good two inches of water on the floor. Water, it turns out, does little to enhance the grip of the linoleum floor and I slipped and skidded into the door, slamming it firmly closed. Brick Shithouse, as I like to remember him, had only taken one step over the threshold, but one wet foot and an even wetter guttersnipe sliding across his floor told him all he needed to know. He was on me in a second, lifting me with one hand and dragging me into the backyard hanging dripping from his grip. He only said three words,

"Ye little cunt!"

I believe he challenged himself to see how many different coloured fluids he could beat out of my body and finally threw me in a soggy, sobbing heap into the alley. Bastard didn't even call the police. Plan A, my arse.

I made my way painfully back to the derelict house which was our base and, seeing the looks of horror on their faces, told Ronnie and Dusty that I'd been set upon by a gang on my way back. Ronnie was on his feet instantly, grabbed a knife from the kitchen and was ready to go and 'hunt those wee fuckers down'. Ronnie had anger issues. Plan B was exactly the same as Plan A, but with one minor change. While waiting for the occupier to return home, I would station myself at the front window of the house, so that I could see who was coming home. It worked a treat. So, once again, at the next house I let the boys go on ahead, while I stayed in the house. I sat nervously at the front window, getting ready to bolt every time I saw a man alone walking up the street. Luckily, they all passed by. Eventually, a man accompanied by a small girl approached the house. I figured that he was unlikely to mete out the same punishment as Brick Shithouse in front of his daughter, so prepared to be caught. The little girl came through the door first, saw me and the wet floor and screamed,

"Da, there's a boy in the house!"

Her father darted past her and before he reached me, I put my hands out pleadingly and said,

"I'm sorry, mister, I'm sorry."

I started to cry, not because I wanted him to feel pity for me, but because I was genuinely remorseful for what I'd done in his house. He told me to sit on the chair in the corner of the room and picked up a poker from beside the fireplace. My heart sank and my arse puckered. Instead of clouting me, he gave the poker to his daughter,

"If he moves from the chair, hit him as hard as you can."

The girl looked as horrified as me, so I tried to give her a look which told her not to worry, as I was going nowhere. There was no phone in the house, so her father ran to the front door, keeping an eye on me over his shoulder.

"Hey, Billy", he called out, "Go down the road and get the coppers. I've got a burglar inside."

I didn't hear any reply, but was relieved that the police would be arriving soon to arrest me. He returned to the sitting room and took the poker from his girl. He looked at me, but I couldn't see any anger in his eyes.

"What are you playing at, son? Are you proud of yourself?"

I don't think he expected an answer and I didn't let him down. I dropped my chin onto my chest and sobbed, feeling very sorry for myself and so, so guilty for what I'd been doing. After a few minutes a policeman arrived, bullet-proof vested with a huge Webley revolver at his side.

"You'll be Johnny, then," he said.

Obviously, Aqua-Thief's reputation had preceded him. After taking some details from the girl's father, he led me out into the street towards his Land Rover. I turned to the man and said,

"I'm really very sorry."

He didn't reply.

Chapter 13 – The System II

We drove through the security checkpoint into the police compound, past the sub-machine gun armed sentries and I was led into the station. There, sitting forlornly on a bench, sat Dusty. He looked up and said,

"Sorry, Johnny."

I opened my mouth to reply and the Sergeant behind the desk shouted at me,

"Shut up, you little fucker. I'll tell you when you can fucking speak!"

I was led into an office and left alone. I couldn't believe it, Dusty had squealed on me, shattering the unspoken code. Wee Bastard. A short time later, a tall, serious man came into the room. He had a large briefcase bursting at the seams with files and papers. He slumped heavily into the chair, probably burdened by having to deal with little shits like me on a daily basis.

"Johnny, I'm from the Welfare. We tried to contact your Da, but he said he didn't want to come in. The police can't interview you without an adult present, so that is why I am here. Do you understand all that?"

Inwardly, I was delighted that my father wasn't there. I nodded and the social worker said,

"You're in a lot of trouble, son. The best you can do now is to tell the truth and don't try to be a smart-arse. The police picked up Alan Rhodes earlier and found some stuff that didn't belong to them.

If You Can't Take a Joke…

The police know that there were three of you running around and when they called Bawnmore, they were told that you were the one who had run away with Wilson and Rhodes."

I interrupted,

"You mean, Dusty didn't squeal on me?"

"No, he didn't. Your pal Wilson managed to get away, but they'll catch him soon enough."

There was very little in the way of process in those days. You got caught, the police told the courts what you did, and the magistrate would find you guilty and sentence you. So much simpler than today, don't you think? I spent my first night in a police cell that evening, having answered all the questions the police had for me. It should have been much more traumatic and I should be reporting my feelings of utter desolation, loneliness and horror at having my liberty taken from me at so young an age. The truth is that I felt none of that. I was given food and for the first night in so long, I slept in on a clean, dry mattress under a snuggly-warm blanket. I didn't wet the bed.

The following morning the police were ready to tell the magistrate what I'd done. Although our cases were to be heard separately, Dusty and I travelled to court together in the back of a police van. As soon as we left the station, the sound of the engine and rattle of the van meant that our words couldn't be heard by the two coppers in the front of the van. Speaking out of the side of my mouth, I asked Dusty how he had been caught. He explained that someone in the vicinity of our derelict house had reported our presence to the local copper and two of them were waiting in the house when he and Ronnie got back.

If You Can't Take a Joke...

The coppers searched them and made them turn out their pockets and found cigarette coupons and a pocket full of shillings, which they correctly assumed came from a gas meter. Dusty told me that he was amazed when Ronnie suddenly started to cry. Ronnie was as tough as they come and wasn't prone to tears. He sniffed to the coppers that he was ashamed of himself and there was more stuff upstairs and,

"Come on up and I'll show you, so I will."

The policemen followed the boys upstairs and into the large room. We had previously ripped up some of the floorboards to burn in the fireplace downstairs. Ronnie went further into the room by balancing on the joists, while the coppers with a firm grip on Dusty's collar stayed safely on the part of the floor which still had floorboards. Ronnie then stopped, turned back to face the officers and set his feet firmly astride two of the joists. He smiled and said,

"Wankers!"

Then he brought his feet together, dropped between the joists and crashed through the lathe and plaster ceiling of the room below. Dusty told me that the sight of two great plodding coppers in bullet-proof vests trying to get down the narrow staircase made him laugh so much that he instantly forgave Ronnie for leaving him behind. As Dusty put it,

"By the time we got into the street, all we saw was a trail of plaster dust settling on the road, just like Wily fucking Coyote!"

My name was read off the court docket and I was accompanied into the courtroom by the same social worker who I'd dealt with the day before. I was to be represented by a Court appointed defence solicitor

If You Can't Take a Joke…

and was led to a seat beside him. He didn't acknowledge me at all and my arse had barely touched my chair, when he suddenly stood up and dug me in the ribs with his elbow to encourage me to do the same. The Clerk of the Court stood and formally read my charge sheet. I was charged with the burglary of the house I was arrested in and had a dozen other offences taken in to consideration. The magistrate, from his raised bench, looked at me over the top of his glasses and asked sternly,

"How do you plead, young man?" I opened my mouth to speak, but the solicitor beside me said,

"Guilty, Your Worship."

The prosecutor, a uniformed police sergeant was invited to outline the prosecution case. He did so with a voice so solemn, that even I started to believe that I was a total and utter little shit, who should be locked up and the key buried under six feet of razor blades. Having completed his character assassination, he sat down, shuffled my file and dropped it onto a pile on the floor. The magistrate looked at me, even more sternly asked,

"Are there any mitigating circumstances?"

Once again the solicitor spoke on my behalf.

"Your Worship, my client has had a difficult childhood, being raised by elderly grandparents, before his father returned from service with the British Army. During the commission of these offences he was a resident of Bawnmore Boys Home."

The magistrate looked at me and thought for a moment. This time he addressed the solicitor directly,

If You Can't Take a Joke…

"Someone should be speaking on his behalf. Where's his father?"

The solicitor referred to his case notes before replying,

"The police contacted him last evening, Your Worship, but he is unable to attend today because he is working."

The magistrate looked angry,

"I am considering a custodial sentence for this young man and before I take such a serious measure, someone ought to say something on his behalf. Fetch his father. I don't care what he's doing, get him in front of me at two o'clock this afternoon."

The last thing I wanted was for my father to speak of me in glowing terms and ask the Magistrate to consider giving me one more chance. I needn't have worried. At two o'clock sharp, we were all back in the courtroom, but this time my father was standing in the witness box. The Magistrate cleared his throat loudly and the whispering and shuffling of papers subdued. He turned towards my father,

"Mr. Wardlow. I should start by saying that I'm surprised and somewhat perturbed that you didn't consider your son's current predicament serious enough to take the morning off work. Given the number of offences committed by your son and the significant damage caused during his spree, I am inclined towards a custodial sentence. Do you have anything to say on your son's behalf?"

My father looked bored and sounded bored, when he replied,

"I've done everything I can, Your Worship. Put him away."

That was it. The last time I'd see him and the last words I'd hear for over 25 years,

"Put him away."

I couldn't have been happier. I was so elated that I can't actually recall what the Magistrate said to me during the sentencing phase. I do remember the last bit, though,

"One to three years in Rathgael."

Chapter 14 – On the Inside

My plan had worked and Dusty, who had also been sentenced to Rathgael, and I were transported the 'school' in a police van. Bangor is a small harbour town on the southern shores of Belfast Lough and was a popular daytripper destination for the residents of a grey and miserable Belfast. I remember being taken there on one of our rare outings during one of my father's leave periods. It had that seaside town smell, a blend of seaweed, damp sand and fish and chips. Rathgael was a mile or two south of Bangor and was considered a dumping ground for children, primarily from the lower socio-economic group, who had been failed firstly by their family and then the welfare system. The residents of Rathgael were incarcerated there for a wide variety of offences and ranged in age from eleven to sixteen years old. Officially it was called Rathgael School, but it was a child prison with no proper schooling, barbed-wire fences and with all dormitories and buildings locked up at night. Those boys who were in Rathgael for persistently truanting, for example, certainly received some schooling, but the curriculum was at a kindergarden level and the real teaching conducted by the more serious offenders. By the time they were released, after up to three years detention, these boys were proficient in smoking, burglary, theft of motor vehicles and assault.

The first stop for new boys was the Reception Block. It was here that we were stripped of all vestiges of our previous lives and the process of institutionalization began. Of course, the first thing I wanted to know was when I could see Fred. I was about to ask one of the staff, but another boy spoke first and I became rapidly discouraged from speaking at all by the sound of an open hand on another boy's cheek and the exclamation,

"This is Rathgael, sonny, you don't speak until you've been spoken to."

I looked around to find the source of the commotion and saw Dusty on the floor with blood dribbling from the corner of his mouth. I recollect thinking that Mr. Smith wouldn't have allowed a staff member at Bawnmore to do that, but before I could develop that thought further, chaos erupted. Dusty slowly got up from the floor and wiped his mouth with the back of his hand. The problem was that the particular staff member who had slapped Dusty didn't know Dusty very well. He didn't know, for instance, that Dusty was sent to Bawnmore because his father had spent three weeks at the Royal Victoria Hospital in traction, after lifting his fist once too often. He also couldn't possibly be expected to know that Dusty's main hobby was fighting. He did it for fun. The staff member had turned his back to Dusty, no doubt confident that he'd taught yet another bloody guttersnipe a useful Rathgael lesson. The red mist consumed Dusty and before anyone could react he swung his leg viciously into the back of the staff's knees, bring him swiftly to the floor. Quickly straddling the man's chest, Dusty became a whirling dervish raining punches and elbows to the hapless guardian's face and head. Despite the guarantee of later punishment, all the boys started jumping and cheering. Nearby staff members rushed to the aid of their associate and dragged Dusty, kicking and screaming, from the chest of their semi-conscious colleague. He was manhandled out of the reception room and I didn't see him again for six months. He was taken immediately to House 4, the high security block, with its unbreakable windows and walled exercise yard.

Rathgael was set up rather like a military establishment, with accommodation blocks and a school building. Not an Alexander, Dill, Alanbrooke or Montgomery to be found here. House 1 was Reception, House 4 the high security block and Houses 2, 3, 5 and 6 were regular blocks. Schooling for Reception and House 4 was conducted within those blocks and the others would march to the school block each morning. Behind Houses five and six was a sports field, although it was out of bounds except when an organized sporting event was taking place and supervised by staff. All meals were prepared and served in the kitchens and dining rooms of each individual House. The Reception Block was designed to ease us gently into the tough regime of Rathgael. We were issued uniforms and introduced to the daily routines. Unlike Bawnmore, the boys did much of the work you'd usually expect to be carried out by adult staff. Cleaning, polishing and washing up the dishes for the twenty or so boys became part of my daily life. The staff members were very strict and adherence to the timetable was paramount. After a couple of days, I finally got to ask whether or not I could see my brother.

"We'd love you to see your brother, Johnny. In fact, we'd love to see him too, but he escaped six weeks ago and has been 'on the run' ever since. Don't you worry, though, wee man, we'll be sure to let you know when he's back."

If You Can't Take a Joke…

I couldn't fucking believe it. I'd run away from Bawnmore, carried out serial burglaries, got the crap kicked out of me, went to court, faced my father for the last time and got sent to Rathgael and all because I wanted to be with my brother. And little fucking Freddie wasn't even there!

After my two weeks of indoctrination, I was assigned to House 5. The head of the house was a wonderful man, Mr. Eric Burns. Mr. Burns was honest, caring, strict and trustworthy, although in retrospect, I feel that he should have done more to stop the more aggressive staff from doling out daily violence to the boys. Burns himself seemed to understand that the boys in his care were not there because they were unsociable, thieves, truants or sociopaths. They were there because of circumstance driven by poverty, neglect, poor parenting or, often, all of the above. That is not to say he was an easy touch. He didn't signal his unhappiness or dissatisfaction with his fists, but rather with his own unhappiness. He was the first person I ever encountered who made me feel bad about what I'd done because of how bad it made him feel. There was a points system in Rathgael, which rewarded good behaviour or success and penalized infractions of the rules. The points were doled out at the weekly House meeting, when the virtues, or otherwise, of all residents were discussed in front of everyone. One of the reasons this points system worked was that the reward was monetary. The higher your 'grading' the more money was put into your account for spending on sweets from the in-house cupboard. Unfortunately, not all staff were as enlightened as Mr. Burns. One particularly nasty member of staff was Mr. Bailey, or

If You Can't Take a Joke…

Judge Bailey as we called him. He was middle-aged, hard-faced and wore his salt and pepper hair swept back from his forehead like Jeff Bridges, but uglier. One day, I had got involved in an argument with a boy called Timmy Higgs about what channel we should watch on television. Both Timmy and I lacked debating skills, so were soon going at each other like a couple of snakes in a bag. Judge Bailey heard the commotion and grabbed us both by the scruff of the neck.

"You pair of little shites don't even know how to fight properly."

Bailey looked at me and said,

"If you want to sort him out, a good punch in the nose will do it. It'll make his eyes water and he won't be able to see you. Watch."

With this, he punched Timmy squarely in the face. His action did, in fact, make Timmy's eyes water but, I think you'll agree, that doesn't make it right. One of the more common inconveniences to the boys, was the constant searches of dormitories. There were usually about ten boys in a dorm, each with a bed and a wardrobe. With monotonous regularity, all the dormitories would be searched for cigarettes. Cigarettes were the black economy of Rathgael. Cigarettes could get you favours, sweets and friends. Fred, before his unscheduled departure was the 'Fag Baron' of House 5. Everyone smoked and I mean everyone. A boy who didn't smoke would be taken aside by his particular House Baron and taught the importance of smoking, how cool it was and that boys who didn't suck cigarettes probably sucked cocks instead. The Baron realizing, of course, that he couldn't control favours, friends or his own position unless everyone was hooked on the evil weed. Cigarettes were acquired in two ways.

If You Can't Take a Joke...

As boys neared the end of their terms, they would be allowed weekend release to visit their families to show them how much they'd changed and how good it would be for all concerned once he returned to the family fold. Upon his return on to Rathgael on Sunday evening, he'd be expected to bring the Baron some fags. All boys were searched by staff prior to being allowed back up to the dorms, so cigarettes had to be smuggled into Rathgael. Some boys were good at this and some, well, not so much. One of the worst was Kenny Hill. I was a very skinny adolescent, but Kenny was a proper runt and also had the heaviest addiction to cigarettes. He was the boy who everyone would get to do the most disgusting things, just for the yuk factor.

"Hey Kenny, I'll give you a fag if you lick my spit of the floor?"

"Kenny, I've got a fag for you. It's in the bathroom, just clean up the mess and it is yours."

In the bathroom, Kenny would find a cigarette sticking out of a turd. In his desperation, he'd take the fag, tear off the shit-covered end and stick it in his pocket for later. Kenny's most memorable attempt to smuggle cigarettes after a weekend home visit was to use masking tape to secure twenty fags individually to his lower legs. Two problems. Although beanpole skinny, Kenny was quite a hirsute youngster and watching him trying to remove masking tapes from his hairy legs was simply gold. The second problem was that the glue used in masking tape does not relinquish its sticky grip on delicate cigarette paper at all. So all Kenny ended up with, for his troubles, were patchy and bleeding legs and a pile of fragments of ex-cigarettes. The most risky method of supplying the Baron involved one of the

If You Can't Take a Joke…

boys breaking out of the facility, buying cigarettes and then returning to the school. Once again, poor Kenny Hill would feature largely in this enterprise, his desire to be popular overriding the threat of punishment and common sense. The plan could only be executed during a sports competition on the playing fields. At any other time we were outside the Houses or school block, we were lined up and marched everywhere, which meant it would be easy to spot if someone went missing. No so during a football match. The sports field was bordered by a small wooded area and as soon as the opportunity presented itself, Kenny would slip into the woods. He then had climb over a barbed-wire topped fence and hike cross country for half a mile to a service station on the A2 road. Having purchased the cigarettes, he would then have to make the return trip and complete the mission before the game was over. Kenny was perfect for this role, as his profile with the staff was very low. It would have been impossible for one of the more notorious boys, Freddie Wardlow for example, as staff watched them like hawks.

Despite the importance of cigarettes as currency, smoking was naturally forbidden. The only time we could smoke was after lights out and lock down. This happened at 8.30pm, when the staff finally went home and the night wardens took over responsibility for keeping the boys safely confined. Security rounds were conducted at irregular intervals, but the wardens simply looked through the inspection window in the door. We'd take it in turns to keep watch at the door, so we'd know when the warden had passed. Once the all clear was given, the security window would be opened to its maximum of about three inches. Three boys would then get a cigarette and would smoke with their faces jammed into the gap, so allowing as much of the smoke as possible to be carried away on the wind. Two or three boys would stand behind the smokers, earning their turn at the window by frantically fanning blankets to ensure that the acrid smell of the tobacco didn't permeate the rest of the house.

Chapter 15 – The Prodigal Brother Returns

It was now that my previously erratic education ground to a halt. After breakfast and morning chores, we would be lined up outside our House and marched up to the School block. The word 'school' appeared to me to be vastly misused within the system. Rathgael was a detention centre, not a school. The School block itself provided little in the way of education, but was a useful facility for keeping large numbers of boys in a controlled environment. The class was made up of boys ranging from eleven to sixteen years old and focused on teaching reading and writing, skills which were lacking in the vast majority of the students. I could read and write very well and was considered quite intelligent and therefore didn't need to participate at all in the 'structured' teaching. There were two of us in this category and we were allowed to self-direct our own education. For the year I spent at school in Rathgael, all I ever did was read. Initially, books would be selected for me with no consideration given to the value of the reading material provided. There was a series of books for primary school children called Janet and John, designed to improve the reading skills of five and six year olds and every Monday a new pile would appear on my desk. I became thoroughly bored and this led to more and more disruptive behaviour. It wasn't until one of House 5's weekly meetings that Mr. Burns recognized that my behaviour was due to boredom rather than belligerence. He asked me how he could help and once I made it clear that the books I was given provided little challenge to me, he ensured that Enid Blyton was replaced by Mark

Twain and Janet and John moved aside in favour of Charles Dickens and Robert Louis Stephenson. The other special boy was Michael Hill, older brother of Kenny, who was a talented young artist. He was provided with art supplies and during my reading year, he did project after project centered around a sheep's skull. He produced drawings, paintings in oil and watercolour and sculptures in clay and papier mache.

After I'd been in House 5 for around two months, Fred was finally recaptured in Belfast and returned to Rathgael. As with all escapees, Fred went straight into House 4 on his return. House 4 held the most disruptive, violent and mentally challenged inmates. Unbreakable windows, impenetrable doors, harsh discipline and violence from both boys and staff was the daily grind of House 4. I was allowed to visit Fred after he'd been back for a couple of days. I was marched into the lobby of the house and searched before being led to the visitor's room. There sat my brother with a huge smile on his face,

"How's about ye, wee man?"

I told him how I had got sent to Rathgael and the fact that the whole plan was based on being with him. He laughed and told me of his escape and escapades. He'd absconded with his mate, Paul Nicholas, after they had been taken to appear in a Belfast court for offences carried out during their previous period 'on the run'. The court had a juvenile waiting room, with about a dozen boys there awaiting their turn for either criminal, welfare or custody hearings. There was a police officer stationed outside the door to ensure that none of the boys tried to flee. From time to time a social worker or

If You Can't Take a Joke…

police officer would come to the room and take boys out when their case was about to be heard. At one point a rather harassed social worker, complete with scruffy jacket and clipboard, appeared in the doorway and queried,

"Kieran and Malachy Elliott?"

No-one moved.

"Kieran and Malachy Elliot," he asked again, slightly impatiently.

Fred quickly realized that the Elliott boys weren't in the room. He nudged Paul Nicholas in the ribs, stood up and said,

"Aye?"

The social worker, who had obviously never met the Elliotts before responded,

"C'mon, you're up."

The police officer at the door was happy to let two of the boys leave the room, as they were accompanied by the social worker. Fred said to the social worker,

"Our Da said he'd be waiting out the front."

The social worker directed impatiently,

"Well don't just stand there, go and fetch him. Court 2. Hurry up."

Fred and Paul casually walked out of the front door to freedom.

Fred then explained that they had made their way to Bawnmore to find me, as the reason he'd broken out in the first place was to see me. At Bawnmore he found out that I had run away with Ronnie and Dusty. He spent the next few weeks scouring all our old haunts around Haypark Avenue totally unaware that I was in the Shankill

Road. Fred had to do three months in House 4, the standard punishment for absconders. Now that Fred was back in Rathgael, albeit securely under lock and key in the high-security block, life became a little easier for me. None of the hard boys would mess with Freddie Wardlow's brother, especially as he would be back in the general population before too long. I continued to smoke, read, sleep, eat and do my chores until Fred finally came back to House 5. He had no intention of staying for too long, though, and next time he went walkies, he was taking me with him. Mr. Burns had received some correspondence from my mother, who was now settled in England and wanted her children back. This wasn't possible given that our detention was court imposed, rather than ordered by the Social Services. We had to do our time.

"Fuck that," said Fred, "I'm over this place. We are going tonight."

Chapter 16 – On The Road Again

Although I had done a runner from Bawnmore and found myself in some odd situations, I wasn't as unreserved or adventurous as Fred and I thought we should quietly see out our time and then join our mother. After all, we only had about three months to wait. As always, Fred won the argument and the escape plan was put in place. That night, as usual, the smokers jammed their faces into the small opening of the window for their nightly puff. Fred jammed his face at the bottom of the dormitory door and blew copious amounts of smoke under the door and into the corridor, knowing that the smell would quickly reach the nostrils of the night warden. Kenny Hill, still game to do anything for a fag, was given a whole cigarette by Fred and stationed in the dormitory at the furthest point from the door. Soon the heavy footsteps of the warden were heard coming down the corridor and everyone jumped into their beds, except for Kenny at the far wall. He stood there and continued to smoke. The warden's eyes filled the inspection window, a small glass slot in the door for checking the boys without having to open it. The warden's concentration was focused on the glowing end of the cigarette. His key grated into the lock and the door swung open.

"Come here, you little bastard!" the warden ordered.

"Fuck off, you old cunt," replied Kenny gamely.

The warden rushed in and Fred and I rushed out, closing the door behind us – a door that was designed to be opened only from the outside. We knew that all the exit doors would be locked, but this didn't bother our Fred.

"You couldn't do this in House fucking 4," he laughed, as he picked up a fire extinguisher and threw it through a plate glass window.

Sirens shrieked and lights flashed informing the wardens at the other Houses that there was trouble afoot. Fred and I were down to the sports field, through the woods, over the fence and 'on the run' while the wardens were still hopping around on one foot trying to get their second legs into their pants. We knew that very soon the police and army would be informed of runners from Rathgael, so we decided not to head north to Bangor because that would be the first place they'd look. It was the closest town, so the closet opportunity to find new clothes, food and shelter. Instead, we headed west towards Belfast. It was a very cold, wet night and that area of County Down is very agricultural, so we made very slow progress across muddy ploughed fields and the occasional farm track. After a few hours, we were cold, miserable and hungry. We finally reached the shore of Belfast Lough at a small village called Holywood, which being exposed to a fresh sea breeze made us even colder. Ahead of us, we saw a compound full of boats, not huge boats, but one or two would certainly provide us with some shelter. We scaled the fence and had a look around. First we checked the club itself to see if there were any open windows, but we were out of luck. We didn't want to risk activating another alarm, so we moved towards the boats. There was a boat in the corner of the yard, which was big enough to require a

If You Can't Take a Joke...

ladder to climb onboard. It had a small varnished door leading down three small steps into its cabin. Fred, far more experienced and adept at life on the run, took charge. He conducted a quick reconnaissance of the area to make sure that the boat could not be seen from the road before switching the lights on inside the boat. The light illuminated a cosy, varnished timber cabin and an inviting double bunk in the bow. There was a small two-burner gas stove, when within seconds of being lit had our faces tingling as the warmth permeated our cold bodies. A cupboard under the stove revealed some dry and canned goods. Neither Fred nor I had ever cooked a proper meal in our lives, but when you are cold and hungry a tin of Heinz Tomato Soup, bulked out with tinned peas and corned beef, then wolfed down with Jacob's Cream Crackers hit the spot. The hot meal and warm cabin soon replaced our previous exhaustion with a comfortable tiredness and we crawled forward into the double bed. We talked, joked and laughed ourselves to sleep. I had not shared a bed with Fred since Grove Street over ten years before, but it felt safe and reassuring being with my brother again.

I awoke next morning to find myself alone in the boat. In a panic, I climbed the small steps into the cockpit, just in time to see Fred dropping from the top of the fence back into the compound. He was carrying a small rucksack that I had seen in the boat the night before. Reaching the bottom of the ladder, he threw it up to me,

"Breakfast time, Johnny," he called up cheerfully.

He had been doorstep shopping and soon the little cooker was called into action once again. Eggs, bread and milk from a neighbouring doorstep combined with corned beef from the boat's larder provided us with a hearty meal to prepare us for the day ahead. Another product of Fred's shopping trip was four or five envelopes, which now lay on the small foldaway table. Back then it was customary to leave payment for the milk, eggs and bread delivered by the milky in an envelope beside that day's empties and Fred had relieved that milky of these payments. We ripped open the envelopes and found, to our delight, one envelope containing five pounds and a note apologizing for being in arrears for so long. With the other envelopes opened, we found ourselves with enough money to survive for a few days with a little left over for necessities like cigarettes. Over breakfast we agreed that we would head to London and live with our mother. We knew the address thanks to her correspondence with Mr. Burns. We had ruled out being able to fly to England because, even if we'd managed to get hold of tickets, the troubles ensured that security at the airport was too stringent for us to get through. We jokingly considered swimming for a while, before getting back to the serious business of planning. There were two main options for getting out of Northern Ireland by sea, namely passenger ferry or freighter. I liked the idea of being stowaways, as this added a Huckleberry Finn flavour to our adventure. Fred had never heard of Huck Finn and informed me that I was not helping. Finally, we determined that passenger ferry was the most logical solution to our crossing the Irish Sea. There were two main options, both of which had pros and cons. The Larne to Stranraer ferry might be easier to obtain tickets for and to get onboard safely, but it would mean having to make our way to London from the

If You Can't Take a Joke…

West Coast of Scotland. The more popular and busy route on the Belfast to Liverpool car ferry, although having tighter security, was nearer to our present location and would result in an easier passage to London at the other end. Once we had decided that the Belfast ferry was our best bet, we then had to decide how to get on to the boat. I suggested that we hide ourselves in the boot of a car or the cargo bay of a truck.

"What? Like Huckleberry Finn, you mean?" asked Fred.

"Yeah, Freddie, exactly like Huckleberry Finn," I answered excitedly.

"Johnny, you read too much," was all he said.

We left the boat before staff started arriving and started walking towards Belfast. We had to be fairly alert, but in these outer suburbs of the city there was not much police or army activity. We had an uneventful journey to Belfast and once men were at work, kids at school and mothers out shopping, we even had time to raid some clothes lines and get rid of our Rathgael outfits. Fred didn't have haute couture tastes, so this took a lot less time than conducting the same exercise with Tab Hunter. With our new clothes our confidence grew and we took a bus the last couple of miles into Belfast City. We couldn't go into the centre of the city itself, as it was by then a traffic free and controlled entry zone. This meant that every street leading to the centre was closed off and the only way in was through and army checkpoint, where thorough searches were conducted. We knew that we didn't have enough funds to cover the ferry fare and also wanted some spare cash, as we didn't like the idea of arriving in England and having to find money before we knew the lie of the land. I was also very unhappy at having to do more burglaries to finance our trip, but Fred had told me not to worry as there was a bloke in Belfast who owed him some money and a couple of favours from the last time he was on the run. I had no idea, still don't as a matter of fact, how Fred had got himself into a position where a grown man owed him money and favours, but it certainly made the next phase of our trip a lot easier. About a mile from where we had found ourselves and close to where we had lived in Haypark Avenue, was the biggest park in Belfast, Ormeau Park. Fred told me to make my way there and he'd see at the front gate in a couple of hours. I only agreed to split up, because Fred insisted that the police in our usual haunts would now know that we were on the run, that there were two of us and that one was Freddie Wardlow, who was well known not just because of his record, but also his shock of white hair. It was now late afternoon and so I could stick to the main roads on my way to the park. Thanks to some of the more progressive schools, uniforms were not always mandatory, so I didn't draw any particular attention to myself in jeans and a jacket and the main roads were less risky than taking my chances with street gangs in the back streets. By the time I reached Ormeau Park, it was dark and a cold, crisp dew was starting to carpet the grass. The park was closed during the dark hours, so I found myself loitering around the entrance outside the rather grand arches and gates. As time passed, army and police patrols increased and I became concerned after one police landrover slowed down and gave me the once over. I was getting colder and colder hanging around in one spot anyway so decided to go into the park. At the side of the main gates was a much lower fence which I climbed over and then moved deeper into the park, the exercise beginning to warm me up. Away from the street lights the shadows became more ominous and I could hear my heart thumping in my chest. Fred and I hadn't agreed a particular time to meet, mainly because neither of us had a watch, so I decided that my best bet was to stay as close to the gate as I could without being seen from the street. The hours dripped by and there was no sign of my brother. By now, a teenager out alone in the street would undoubtedly draw the attention of any patrol which caught sight of him, so I stayed hiding in a clump of bushes peering out into the street. I started to imagine all the things which might mean that Fred wouldn't be coming and I'd be alone again. He could have been recognized by police if he'd gone back to his old haunts, or been picked up by a random patrol. There was also the possibility that he'd been intercepted by one of the paramilitary organizations and was attending a kangaroo court as I hid in the bushes. Suddenly there was a rustle in the trees right behind me and a hand thumped firmly onto my shoulder. I nearly parted company with my skin, then Freddie's voice scolded,

"You're really shit at this, our John."

We moved out of the bushes and I could see Fred's face split by a huge smile.

"How'd you know where I was hiding?" I asked.

He placed his hands on both of my shoulders and turned me around to face the park. There, as clear as day, lay my footprints on the dewy grass leading straight into the bushes.

It was now too late to do anything, as being in the open wasn't an option. The park was bordered by the Ormeau Embankment, which ran alongside the river Lagan and just inside the park fence was a toilet block, the only shelter in the park. For a professional like our Fred, the security presented no problems and soon we were inside and settling down for the night. Fred had returned to Ormeau with a small backpack and as we sat on the cold tiles, he produced a bottle of lemonade and some biscuits, which were scoffed down as we discussed what to do the next morning. We now had cash and although our nostrils were being assailed by a heady combination of stale urine from the toilet block and the claggy odour of the Lagan River not 30 yards away, we were safe for the moment. We talked, planned and smoked ourselves to sleep.

Chapter 17 – Over the Water

After a night's sporadic sleep, we awoke early. We couldn't leave the park until there were more people about, so we made our way back to the hiding place in the bushes near the gates. Overnight rain had obliterated my footsteps and Fred was kind enough not to mention the fact. We sat in the bushes, finishing off the lemonade and biscuits and watched the city come to life. The frequency of the Belfast City Corporation Buses increased as the rush hour approached and soon the gates to the park were unlocked and it was time for us to leave and head towards the docks. It was about four miles away, but it was a typical grey, drizzly and miserable day, so we decided to take the bus. Again, Fred decided that we shouldn't travel together, so when the first bus approached down Ormeau road, I dashed across and got onboard. I looked back towards the park entrance as the bus drove onto the bridge over the river and saw our Fred sitting on the low park wall puffing on a fag. How come when I was with him, he always appeared so big and strong, but from the bus all I saw was a white-haired adolescent who looked as small and vulnerable as I felt? The bus trips passed uneventfully and we were soon reunited fairly close to the dockyard. There was a military checkpoint in operation at the entrance, controlling both access to and exit from the ferry port. A couple of bored looking soldiers were conducting cursory checks of those going into the ferry port, but the main focus of attention was on those arriving into Belfast. The Belfast-Liverpool ferry carried both passengers and vehicles and it was the vehicles arriving into the city

If You Can't Take a Joke...

which warranted most scrutiny, as the priority of the day was halting illegal arms shipments. We noticed that when the backlog of vehicles trying to get out of the dockyard increased, one of the soldiers posted at the entry was generally seconded to help at the exit. We still had to get passed the single sentry and we knew that two young teenagers travelling by themselves would draw unwanted attention. As usual, Fred had the answer. A dockworker, complete with green overalls and company emblem on his breast pocket was approaching and Fred spoke to him.

"'Scuse me, mate. Me and my brother are going to Liverpool to stay with our Granny and watch the match at the weekend, but we probably won't get into the docks by ourselves. Can you take us in with you?"

At the same time, he waved a couple of crisp one pound notes under the nose of the dockie, indicating that we'd make it worth his while and that no further explanation should be sought. The worker clearly knew that we were either runaways, criminals or, at the very least, just a pair of wee shites, but two quid is two quid and he snapped up the notes from Fred's outstretched hand saying,

"No problem, boys, come with me."

We joined the queue at the entrance and when we reached the sentry, the dockie held up his ID.

"Alright there wee man," he said cheerfully to the young soldier, "I'm just taking my nephews to the boat. They're off to Liverpool on tonight's ferry, jammy wee bastards, so they are."

The sentry paid little attention to us,

If You Can't Take a Joke…

"Have they got tickets?"

Our 'Uncle' told him that he was taking us straight to the ticket office to pick them up. We were waved through without a second glance. Fifty yards into the ferry port, the dockie said,

"I'd better come with you and get your tickets. I don't need to know your business, lads, but you'll be better off buying return tickets even if you're not coming back. Less suspicious, y'know. You got cash?" Fred gave him enough money to cover the cost of the tickets and the cost of a pint or two. About ten minutes later we bade farewell to Uncle Dockie and we had return tickets on that evening's ferry stowed in our pockets and were sitting in the terminal with a cup of tea and bacon roll. We had a nervous few hours waiting for boarding time to arrive, but as the terminal gradually filled up with passengers we managed to relax a little. At around 8.30pm that evening the public address system announced that passengers for that night's sailing should make their way to the departure gate and Fred and I joined the line. Our tickets were checked and in a few minutes we were aboard the ferry settling down in a couple of reclining chairs ready to doze off and wake up in England. About thirty minutes prior to sailing one of the ship's crew came through the passenger lounge and starting checking tickets. He moved quickly through the lounge checking tickets and chatting with the passengers. Our turn came,

"Travelling by yourselves, lads?"

I explained that we were big Liverpool fans and were staying with our Granny until the match on Saturday.

"Very nice, boys. Hey, let's hope that Peter Osgood has a good game, eh?"

I tried to look confident,

"Yeah, I'm sure he will."

The crewman went off and continued his ticket checking and chatting. Fifteen minutes to go and we'd be on our way. We knew that there'd be little checking of foot passengers at the English terminal and were confident that we'd be having breakfast in Liverpool. With ten minutes to go our nerves got the better of us.

"Let's go and find somewhere a bit quieter," suggested Fred and we got up to leave.

At the door of the lounge, the ticket checker was pointing to us and from behind him emerged a policeman. I looked over my shoulder and saw another copper at the only other exit from the lounge. We sat down. The police officer made his way down the aisle between the rows of seats and stopped beside us,

"Hello, Freddie. Remember me?"

"Yes, sir, I do." Fred replied miserably.

The police officer looked at me,

"Ah, Johnny. Ah, Johnny. Any real Liverpool fan would know that Peter Osgood plays for Chelsea." Fred looked at me,

"Oh yeah, our John, we're huge fans, so we are."

The two police officers escorted us from the boat and we were taken to the security office to await transport back to Rathgael. I couldn't believe our atrocious luck. Ten minutes from getting totally away and we get busted because of Peter fucking Osgood. I was close

If You Can't Take a Joke...

to tears, but Fred, who had an incredible knack of taking things in his stride, just looked at me and said,

"Don't worry, wee man, next time, eh?"

We were back in Rathgael by about midnight. Given the lateness of the hour, we were bedded down in a dormitory in the Reception Block and after breakfast the following morning were taken to see Mr. Burns in House 5. This was unusual, as returned escapees were usually taken straight to the high security block, House 4. We were marched down to house 5 and taken to the main office. For some reason, Mr. Burns liked Fred, despite the fact that he was a trouble-maker, persistent absconder, thief and all-round smart-arse. In turn, Mr. Burns was the only person in authority that Fred respected.

"I'm going to miss you, Freddie," he said, as he took his seat behind his desk.

He reached down to the floor beside his desk and hoisted up a brown paper parcel neatly tied with string. In bold black letters, it said simply "Fred Wardlow". Upon arrival at Rathgael, everything you have is taken away, wrapped in brown paper and returned to you only on your final departure. I looked at Fred and he looked at me, both of us knowing that this meant he was being sent to Missile, a tougher borstal situated further from Belfast and with a fearsome reputation.

"Mr. Burns, will our Johnny be coming with me?" enquired Fred.

"Yes, but not for a few weeks until his time here is up."

I was crushed and sobbed,

"Mr. Burns if I'm going to Millisle anyway, why can't I go at the same time as our Fred? I only got into trouble so that I could come here and be with him."

Mr. Burns suddenly laughed, somewhat inappropriately I thought.

"Boys, boys, you're not going to Millisle, you're going to live with your mother in England!"

For the first time, I saw my wise-cracking, smart-arse brother speechless. I wasn't much better and could only gibber,

"What? I mean, how…."

Mr. Burns explained that our mother had been in constant contact with him for some time, but he didn't say anything to us because he didn't want to build our hopes up. Fred, like me, had been sentenced to one-to-three years and had completed well over two years, so was eligible for immediate release, provided that he had a Social Security approved place to live. I, on the other hand, hadn't quite reached the one year point and as my confinement was court ordered, the Social Services could not approve my release. My mother had petitioned the Home Secretary for my early release, but the wheels of bureaucracy grind even more slowly than the wheels of justice and it was likely that my year would pass before a decision was made. Mr. Burns went on to explain that my mother and her new man-friend, as he called him, had actually arrived in Northern Ireland the day after we had gone on the run. The plan was that we would both be released into their care for a couple of days to help become reacquainted and then I would come back to Rathgael for a month or so and Fred would go off to England with them. Mr. Burns laughed again,

"So Freddie, while you were busy trying to catch a boat to England, sure your mother is just down the road with airplane tickets!"

More serious now, he said,

"Boys, I know about the boat in Holywood and I've had a chat with the owner. He told me that you didn't do any damage, so he won't be pressing charges. Your mother has already taken a little drive over there to deliver a proper 'bottle' of thank you. Now, are there any more incidents that I should know about? I don't want to be having to drag either of you back from London, so if there is anything else tell me now."

For once, we could honestly reply that we hadn't done any burglaries. We instinctively thought it wise not to mention stealing food and cash from doorsteps, stealing clothes or criminal damage to the door of the Ormeau Park toilets. We'd raided enough doorsteps and clothes lines to require a boot-full of 'bottles' of thank you.

"Okay, boys, your mother and Mr. Skull are downstairs waiting for you," said Mr. Burns signaling the end of our meeting.

"Skull?" said Fred, "Are you serious? Nobody is called Skull, Mr. Burns."

Burns smiled,

"Unusual indeed, Freddie, but Skull it is."

We followed Mr. Burns down into the common room, which was quiet as all the boys had already been marched up to the school block. Fred and I hesitated at the bottom of the stairs and Mr. Burns nudged us forward deeper into the room, before making himself scarce. My mother was sitting on a chair beside the window and standing beside her was a young-looking man, Mr. Skull. He cleared his throat to draw my mother's attention to our arrival. She looked around and saw her boys standing there in Rathgael uniforms. She caught her breath and could only say,

"My boys, my wee boys," before running to us, dropping to her knees and holding us as close as we could get without actually being behind her.

Tears started to well up in my eyes, but I caught a look from Fred, which clearly implied that I should keep it together. With some difficulty, my mother pulled herself together, but still clung to our hands.

"Boys, this is Alan and you'll be living with us and Caroline in England."

My only previous experience with new people in my parents' lives was with the 'Aunties' who frequented Haypark Avenue and I suppose I was suspicious from the outset. Alan looked at us and smiled,

"Boys, you are making your mother a very happy woman and that makes me happy, so thanks very much."

He didn't overdo it, didn't approach us and, thankfully, didn't offer us his hand to shake. I suppose he was smart enough to know that there was no point in trying to win us over, so to speak, as we had had enough experience with grown-ups to recognize when someone was trying too hard. He just stayed slightly behind our mother and let her take the lead. Just then, Mr. Burns returned to the common room with a tray laden with cups of tea and a plate of chocolate biscuits.

The five of us took seat around a table and Mr. Burns poured the tea. He offered the plate of biscuits to my mother,

"From my own stock, Mrs. Wardlow. We don't give the boys too much chocolate as it has a tendency to make them a little over active!"

The three adults exchanged small talk – the weather, flight details and that sort of thing, while Fred and I sat silent, contributing nothing. My head was still spinning. In the last twenty four hours, I'd woken up in a public toilet, bribed a dockie to get us into the dockyard, actually boarded the Belfast-Liverpool ferry, got nicked again and returned to Rathgael. Now it appeared that instead of having at least two years left here, in a matter of weeks I would be living in England with my mother, new 'daddy', Freddie and my sister Caroline. Bloody Hell.

Chapter 18 – The Skull Family

Just as Mr. Burns had promised, Fred and I left Rathgael that day to spend a couple of days with our mother and Alan before they dropped me back at Rathgael and headed off to England. I remember it was a strained couple of days, probably because everything was so alien to Fred and me. We stayed, for the first time in our lives, in nice hotels. Alan obviously had more money that we had ever experienced and had hired a car. No trains or buses anymore, but travelling in style in a Ford Cortina, spending most of our time on our knees looking out of the back window. My mother was trying very hard not to stare at us and Alan was the only one who was being normal. He was like no one I had ever met before and sounded like one of the English actors off the telly. He told really bad jokes, so bad that you had to laugh and he would talk to everyone we met. I am not sure he was fully cognizant of how unpopular English people were in some parts of Northern Ireland back then, or maybe he was just bluffing. Of course, these couple of days didn't pass entirely without incident. One of our day-trips included a visit to the beach at Bangor and our sister Caroline had joined us. It was a sunny day and as we strolled along the promenade, Alan pointed to a kiosk across the road and asked if anyone fancied an ice-cream. Caroline and I responded with 'ooh, yes pleases', however, Fred simply dashed across the road in the direction of the kiosk. The rest of us looked on in horror as, unlike Fred, we had seen the car that was closing in on him at a rapid rate of knots. A screech of skidding tyres and a yelp from Fred followed. Mum screamed and Alan dashed

If You Can't Take a Joke…

over to where Fred lay, took off his jacket and formed a pillow, which he placed under Fred's head. An ambulance was summoned and we followed it in the car to the local hospital. Caroline and I were told to stay in the waiting room, as Mum and Alan escorted Fred into the treatment area. We knew that he wasn't seriously hurt, because he was sitting up on the gurney, as Mum held his hand. Caroline looked at me and sighed,

"I was going to have strawberry flavor with a Flake!"

Shortly afterwards, Alan stuck his head around the treatment room door,

"Fred's fine, do you want to come and see him?"

We stood up and went through the door to see Fred sitting bolt upright on the gurney with a grin like a Cheshire cat…and the biggest bowl of ice-cream I'd ever seen. Bastard!

After a couple of days of driving, cafes and general sightseeing, it was time for me to return to Rathgael to await either a response from the Home Secretary or the arrival of the first anniversary of my detention. The last few weeks passed in a daze. My main concern was to stay out of trouble or at least not get caught. I whiled away my days reading at the back of the class and wondering what school would have in store for me in England. I was approaching fifteen and this was the legal minimum age to finish school in Northern Ireland, so I really only had a couple of months to go before I could be unleashed into the world. My last week in Rathgael slowly crept by and, finally, on the day of my first anniversary at Rathgael, Mr. Burns took me up to his office.

If You Can't Take a Joke...

"Well, Johnny, today's the day. I've got your ticket and we'll find someone to take you to the airport and you'll be in London before you know it," he smiled.

As I sat there in his office, dressed smartly in the clothes my mother had sent over from England for me with my brown paper parcel on my lap, I realised that of all the people that I'd met, Mr. Burns was the only man who I'd known for any length of time who cared about me. Sure, there was the social worker who got me off the streets and into Bawnmore and although I can only think of him in kind terms, that was a short term commitment. Mr. Burns had looked after me for a year, tolerated my belligerence and forgave my indiscretions. Despite having the authority and endless justification, he never lifted his hand to me, unlike many of the staff, particularly that bastard Judge Bailey. Eric Burns looked at me with some concern,

"Johnny, you are being presented with a great opportunity and I hope that you'll grasp it with both hands. You are a smart boy and it is time you started using that brain of yours. You've not had a great start, but never let that be an excuse for not succeeding in life."

I stood up, hugged Mr. Burns and dropped the brown paper parcel into a waste bin. The only thing Irish that I took to England was my accent.

By four o'clock that afternoon, I was in my new home at Stonechat Close, Ferndown, Dorset. The contrast with Grove Street and Haypark Avenue made me giddy. I still shared a room with our Fred, but instead of being huddled together under army greatcoats, we had our own beds and cupboards. In reality, it was a fairly modest house in a fairly modest neighbourhood, but to us it was a different world. Neatly mown lawns replaced the red, white and blue painted kerbstones and there were trees. We even had a huge one at the back of our house at the bottom of the garden — a garden complete with grass. Alan worked hard as an executive for a large insurance company and we really wanted for nothing. He maintained the tradition of having a room that was out of bounds for the kids unless he was in it. He had a new Bang and Olufsen stereo, his pride and joy, and I can still remember my amazement the first time I heard a stereo recording. I closed my eyes and was convinced that the orchestra was in the same room with me. There were still domestic arguments — we were after all a house with two adults, three teenagers and our new younger brother, Steven. Steven was the carrot-topped product of another of Mum's liaisons about five years previously, but had come as part of the package deal Alan had accepted when he fell in love with my mother. I don't think Steven was particularly enamoured by his new family and to Fred and I, who had done some hard yards, he appeared a spoilt brat. The family arguments were verbal and although they could be quite aggressive at times, physical violence at home was no longer part of our lives.

Although my fortunes had improved enormously, thanks to Alan's courage and his love for my mother, there was still the challenge of settling down in a new country. Although part of the United Kingdom family, Northern Ireland was rather like the drunk uncle at a wedding, or the ginger-haired stepchild. It turned out, though, that

English teenagers were no different to their Irish cousins – selfish, stroppy and cliquey. Fred dealt with this by managing to find the most selfish and stroppy clique and happily joined them in their mischief! He was also still fairly handy with his fists and would sometimes vent his frustration with life by picking fights with me. He was always bigger than me and I would too often be his punching bag. I, on the other hand, no longer wanted to be the outcast skirting the law, authority and the social mores of middle-class Ferndown. I wanted to go to school and get qualified for university. So, with Rathgael behind me and dreams of University rattling around my head, a final note on Rathgael, my 'school' during the most important and formative years of my education.

In 2015, Rathgael became the subject of the Northern Ireland Historical Institutional Abuse enquiry and the subsequent report in 2017 noted that Rathgael:

- Accommodated the most difficult, damaged, disturbed and, in some cases, delinquent children from the Protestant communities of Northern Ireland
- The practice of using frequent unrecorded informal corporal punishment was unacceptable, amounting to systematic abuse
- The failure to prevent bullying by peers amounted to systemic abuse

Testimony from one former 'resident' included the following statement:

- "I have been permanently scarred by my experience at Rathgael. The children were brutal and the staff turned a blind eye. I lived in fear of everyone around me and was beaten by both children and staff."

They did not have to spend millions of pounds on this enquiry…they could have just asked me!

Chapter 19 – Work Experience

One of the problems I encountered was my harsh, rattling Belfast accent. I moved to England in early 1974 and this was also the time when the IRA had shifted their campaign of violence over the Irish Sea to the mainland. Bombings in Birmingham and London did little to further my own campaign to settle down and be a good boy. My accent made people suspicious of me and more than once I'd be accused of terrorism and invited to go back where I came from. A few times, it went further than harsh words and I had to learn to be either quick on my feet or with my fists. After a few failed attempts at using my fists, I figured out that my feet were more advantageous to my survival and I became quite the sprinter!

I was to attend Ferndown Upper School, which was a modern facility having opened only three years before. Joining any school in the middle of the academic year poses problems for both students and schools. As my history was known to the headmaster, his obvious assumption was that I would leave school as soon as possible and that it was pointless expending any energy or resources towards my education. On my first morning, I received no encouragement to study, no questions as to whether I wanted to take 'O' Levels or if I had any aspirations whatsoever regarding further education. I was offered the Job Experience program. This program is purportedly designed to help the less academically inclined students to assimilate into the workforce. I had actually been looking forward to kick-starting my education and was devastated by the implication that I wasn't worth the school's effort. I had never studied woodwork or metal work, so my opportunities, even in the school sponsored work experience program, were limited. Factories wanted boys who had shown promise in the practical courses, as they often made cheap, but willing apprentice fodder. I was offered a position in a green grocer's fruit and veg shop. The shop was typical of the day, with crates of fresh produce tiered in the street in front of the shop. At the back of the shop was the storage area leading out to a car park. Gordon, the owner, was a grumpy old bastard, who continually claimed that he couldn't understand a word I was saying. The only reason he kept me on after the first day is because I was even better than cheap labour – I was free. This was my first real job, but within a week I was fired. It wasn't that I didn't try hard, nor was it because I hated it or even Grumpy Gordon. It was simply bad luck. Part of my job was to fill boxes with customers' fruit and veg orders for delivery later by Gordon. I'd be given a list for a pound of carrots, a pound of onions, etc. and would load up a box and put the customer's name on top and then load the box into the van, an old Commer with a huge sliding door along the side. It was my third day and I was busy packing the orders and loading the van, which was parked about twenty yards away, directly behind the shop. It had started to rain heavily and I was getting cold, wet and more miserable with every load. It would be so much easier if the van was closer, I decided. The fact that I didn't have a driving licence or, more importantly, the ability to drive did not deter me. It couldn't be that hard, could it? Fortunately, the van was on an incline which sloped down towards the shop. This meant that I would not even have to start the engine. All I had to do was ease off the handbrake, let the van roll gently towards the shop and then apply the handbrake again. I eased myself into the driver's seat and carried out some checks. First I made sure that Gordon wasn't around. Check. Then I made sure that what I thought was the handbrake was in fact the handbrake by slowly releasing it and then quickly pulling in back on. Check. No obstacles between the van and the desired stopping point. Check. I jumped back out of the van to see if the wheels were pointing straight ahead. Check. Back in the driver's seat, I ever so gently, inch by inch, released the hand brake. The van gave a little squeak as it moved forward in a straight line. I fully released the brake and forward momentum built. We'd gone about ten yards when I realized that the incline was steeper than I thought, so I rapidly pulled the handbrake upwards. My hand didn't stop until it was above my head, still holding the handbrake lever with a broken cable dangling from the end. The van continued to increase speed towards the back of the shop. I had no idea which pedal worked the brakes, but quickly developed a plan. As soon as the van hit the boxes of fruit and vegetables, I would jump out, grab a box and declare as soon as Gordon appeared that the van had suddenly rolled towards me and he was lucky I wasn't injured. I even had the door open ready for the impact. When it came, the impact was much fiercer than I had imagined and when the van crashed into the shop, I was thrown forward. My head slammed into the middle of the steering wheel, exactly where the horn button sat. Boy, that was one noisy horn! I jerked back and saw Gordon, alerted by the cruiser-liner blast of the horn, dashing from inside the shop. He didn't say anything at all. He just looked at me and waved his hand with a clear message that I should leave and never darken his doorstep again.

My next work experience was with a company call Purewell Electrical, who since my time with them have grown considerably into a large retail company. Back then, they had a small workshop in Purewell, Christchurch and specialized in television repairs. My job was to remove the back covers of the televisions and then vacuum out the built up dust before passing it to the technicians to carry out the repairs. One morning, there was a delivery of about 30 television sets of the same model, all recalled by the manufacturer due to faulty channel change mechanisms. This was during the days when you had to get off your lazy arse and go to the TV set to change channel, as remote controls were still not common. So there I was faced with a vanload of sets to be vacuumed. I had completed this by around lunchtime and could do nothing else because there was no room to move until the button mechanism was changed. The new controls had already been delivered by the manufacturer, but for some reason the technician was not at work that day. I had a look at the problem and, through boredom rather than anything else, removed the old controls from the first set and replaced it with the new equipment. I plugged in the television and it worked. It was not exactly rocket science, but it was the first time I can remember actually fixing something. Within a couple of hours, I had completed all of them. The manager of the company came back into the workshop and saw that the televisions had their back panels on them.

"How come these aren't done?" he asked.

"They are done," I replied. "It is a bit daft to take the cover off, clean them and put the covers back on before they're fixed, isn't it?"

I explained what I had done and he frantically test two or three of the televisions.

"You are kidding me! It normally takes a day just to change out the controls. Excellent!"

He took out his wallet and gave me five pounds.

"If you can work like that, you ought to be paid. Bugger the school."

He called the manufacturer and told him to pick up the television sets and drop off another thirty. What I didn't know at the time, was that he called the technician who had taken a 'sickie' and told him not to come back. I was given increasingly complex tasks to do and the manager took a great deal of care explaining exactly what needed to be done and I learned a lot from him. He started to pay me, cash in hand as I was officially on work experience and too young to earn a wage, and suddenly I had money in my pocket and felt that I was doing something worthwhile.

Apart from working at Purewell, I didn't do much of anything else. Because I didn't go to school, I didn't make any friends and I was too young to socialize with the staff at work. I stayed in my room and read book after book. Fred was out every night and was falling back into some of his old habits. He was also supposed to be on work experience, but he refused to work for anyone for free. He didn't go to school, but hung around with some of the other dropouts from the area. Shoplifting, burglary and general bastardry filled his days and, once again, he came to the attention of the police. He got lucky and always managed to find an alibi or talk his way out of trouble. Finally, August came and Fred and I turned sixteen years old and officially entered the world of work. The manager at Purewell was not allowed to keep me on, as this was in contravention of the work experience scheme and he would have lost his chance at being on the list for free employees. I was quite happy, as the commute to Purewell was long and usually cold and wet. For our sixteenth birthday, Alan had paid the deposit on two Batavus mopeds. Bright orange, 50c.c. of throbbing engine and a maximum speed of 30 miles per hour – downhill and with a tail wind. We kicked the starters over on the driveway and the smile split my face in two as the engine burst into life. Helmets on and then we were ning-ning-ninging our way down the road. The junction was about 100 yards away and I stopped, as required by law, self-preservation and common sense. Fred, right behind me, had no respect for the law, thought he was invincible, had no common sense and couldn't find his brakes, so used me and my moped instead. Down I went and so did my rear tire. Alan, still standing at the end of the drive, must have been wondering what he had done.

Now it was time to get a proper job. Resumes and cover letters were not as prevalent in the mid-70s as they are today. Finding a job involved knocking on the doors of all the factories in the industrial estates around Ferndown. I did this for days on end and found that my size, I was only about five feet five inches tall and seven stone soaking wet, and my accent were barriers to employment. Finally, I got to see a Mr. Brown, the personnel manager at the Max Factor plant in Wallisdown just a couple of miles from home. My interview lasted about thirty seconds.

"What are you like with heights?" he enquired.

"No problem, Mr. Brown," says I.

"Right, go and see Wilf in the storeroom," he said, gesturing in the general direction of the storeroom. I walked unescorted through the noisy factory floor with its sorting, filling, wrapping and stacking machines and the dizzying smell of Max Factor perfume mixed with lubricating oil. Trying hard to avoid being run over by motorized palette trucks, I asked one of the machine operators where the storeroom was. He examined me for a moment, obviously trying to determine any signs of intelligence and having failed said,

"Behind the fucking sign with Storeroom on it, dummy!"

He indicated behind me and there, not 10 feet away, was a large sign indicating my goal. Shit. I knocked loudly on the door and a voice shouted,

"Hatch!"

This meant nothing to me, so I knocked again.

"Fucking Hatch!"

Still at a loss, I knocked for the third time. The door was flung open and an old man in a brown coat stood there. I started,

"My name's John and Mr. Brown told me to come and see you, 'cause I'm going to be your new assistant storeman." I was silenced by a raised hand.

"Fucking hatch! If you want to speak to me, come 'round to the fucking hatch," he sighed, indicating a serving hatch on the opposite wall of the store. He slammed the door.

Bloody hell, I didn't even know if this was Wilf. I walked quickly all the way around the large storeroom and found myself at the hatch. The old man had mysteriously beaten me there.

"My name's John and Mr. Brown told me to come and see you, 'cause I'm going to be your new assistant storeman."

"Well, why didn't you say so, young fellah. Come on round and I'll let you in."

I retraced my path all the way back around the store and there was Wilf standing beside the open door gesturing me to enter the store. Unsure as to what to say next, I thrust my right hand forward,

"John Wardlow, pleased to meet you, Sir."

"I'm Wilf. Welcome to my domain," replied Wilf, grasping my hand with his left hand and leading me deeper into 'his domain'- effectively holding hands.

My mind flashed back to my early days on the streets of Belfast and the stories of strange men who were nice to you and then fiddled with you. I pulled my hand away and was about to run for my life, when I glanced down and saw that Wilf did not actually have a right hand. He laughed,

"Don't worry, mate. Catches a lot of people out."

He waved his hook in front of my face and made it open and close and I laughed with him. He sat me down behind a desk and had me fill in some forms for the personnel department, because Human

Resources had not been invented yet. When I had finished the forms, he said,

"Right first things first. A nice cup of tea. I'll make this one, but after this it's your job, right?"

"Sure thing, Wilf."

Over a cup of hot sweet tea, Wilf explained that Mr. Brown was looking for someone to take over as Head Storeman when he retired the following year.

"One day, all this will be yours," said Wilf dramatically, waving his hook over the entire store.

Chapter 20 – Apprentices and Apprehension

The storeroom contained every spare component required to keep all areas of the factory running at full capacity. Nuts, screws, bolts, fuses, O-rings, gaskets, switches, tubing, widgets and wotsits were held in massive rows of floor to ceiling shelving. Mr. Brown's only interview question about heights was because many of the less in demand items were kept at the top of the racks and required me to climb around thirty feet up a ladder, which looked like it had seen service in the trenches. Wilf, who had lost his hand during the war, was remarkably dexterous with his hook, but climbing up and down the ladder at his age with only one hand was effectively impossible. All day and every day, heads would appear at our hatch with a requisition form and Wilf would complete the paperwork while I scuttled around the racks like a powder monkey on a sailing ship collecting the necessary spares. The Max Factor facility was home to a lot of apprentices. There were fitters, toolmakers, mechanical engineers and electricians all at various stages of their three-year apprenticeships. It was common practice to play pranks on these youngsters as part of their 'education'. Requisitions for skyhooks, glass hammers, left-handed screwdrivers and spare bubbles for spirit levels were commonplace, however, often more elaborate pranks were played. A young fitter would appear with a requisition form for a 'long stand' and Wilf would tell him,

"We got a few of those. Which model do you need?"

If You Can't Take a Joke...

The apprentice would hurry back to his foreman and reappear after a few minutes,

"I need a one slash two H R stand, please."

Wilf would instruct him to write the model number on the form and the lad would duly write, '1/2 HR' and was told to wait. Wilf and I would sit down and have a cup of tea, while the apprentice stood at the hatch growing increasingly impatient, as we did nothing to fill his order. After about 30 minutes, Wilf would go to the hatch and say,

"Ok, lad, that should do it. Off you go."

Baffled, the apprentice would ask,

"But what about my stand?"

"All done," said Wilf pointing to the requisition form, "It says here you wanted a half hour long stand and you've been standing there for 30 minutes!"

We also kept a tin of shoe polish in the store. It had a slight indentation in the polish into which we'd syringe a drop of water. When an apprentice appeared with a requisition for a new bubble for a spirit level, he'd be handed the tin of polish with the new bubble sitting in the middle and informed that this was the last one we had, so he'd better be bloody careful. He would set off towards his department with the concentration of a surgeon and the speed of a slug. Happy days.

As I gained experience in the running of the store, Wilf started to take a back seat and he would while away his days reading the paper or filling in his football pools. He had worked in this store for nearly thirty years and was looking forward to retirement. Soon, I knew all

If You Can't Take a Joke...

there was to know about the store and became increasingly bored with the same routine day after day. One day, my first customer was a young apprentice requesting a dozen 2BA bolts and as I handed him the brown paper bag and slid the clipboard over to him for his signature, the thought struck me that I was just like him. Sixteen years old and just starting out on my working life. Then a qualified fitter appeared with an order for a couple of gaskets. I slid the clipboard to him and thought that this could be me in ten years. Better paid and established in the factory. A foreman was next and I started to panic. He was in his mid-thirties with a responsible job and probably had a wife and kids at home. Was this me in twenty years? Next came Mr. Brown, mid-forties, on his weekly personnel rounds. At the end of the day, my head was in a spin. Wilf stood up from his desk, shrugged off his brown coat and slipped on his jacket,

"I'm heading off, John. I'll leave you to lock up. G'night."

As I watched him shuffle down the factory aisle, a voice screamed in my head,

"THAT IS YOU IN FIFTY YEARS!"

Chapter 21 – Into the Blue

It was a typical cold, drizzly September evening as I jumped onto my faithful Batavus moped that evening to ride the short distance to my home. The frantic panic over my future had become a curtain of gloom, as I brought my orange steed to a stop at a set of traffic lights. I do not know if it was fate, coincidence or pure luck, but on a large advertising hoarding beside the road sat two large posters. One was for some car or other, but the one, which grabbed my immediate attention, was a recruitment poster for the Royal Navy. A happy looking sailor under a clear sunny sky, cap at a jaunty angle and a simple slogan:

"JOIN THE NAVY AND SEE THE WORLD"

I think I made the decision then and there. I was bored with the factory, I was bored at home and I had no friends. I raced home at 29 miles per hour, suddenly filled with excitement and with visions of sunning myself on a faraway beach, surrounded by native beauties bringing me drinks in a coconut. I got home and started to compile, in my head, everything I knew about the organization that was about to change my life. It didn't take long. Most of what I imagined was gleaned from movies, in particular the Noel Coward timeless epic 'In Which We Serve'. I was not naïve enough to envision myself as an officer like Coward's Captain Kinross, but could certainly relate to Ordinary Seaman Shorty Blake, played by John Mills. Also, I thought I'd look quite good in blue. I was desperate to learn more about the organization, but the libraries were closed and in 1974 Google was just a noise made by babies. Alan had a 30-volume set of Britannica Encyclopedia and I snatched Volume RAT-RUK, or whatever, from the bookshelf. The fascinating 1000-year history of the Royal Navy engrossed me for hours and by the time I had finished cross-referencing, about 10 volumes of the Encyclopedia lay strewn across the floor. NAT-NUK revealed the life and career of Lord Nelson, TAT-TUK detailed his victory at Trafalgar and FAT-FUK covered what he did in his spare time with Lady Emma Hamilton. Later that evening, I told Alan and my mother about my new career choice, hoping that they would be as excited as I was. My mother complained that she only just had me back and now I was going to run off and join the navy. Alan told me that I would never get in because of my criminal record and that as I was only sixteen, my mother would have to sign her consent and she was not likely to do that, so maybe I should wait until I was eighteen. I was devastated at the lack of support and I could feel the burn of tears welling up in my eyes. I pulled myself together, refusing to cry. I insisted that this was going to happen whether they thought it was a good idea or not. They left me alone with my anger. After my mother had gone to bed, Alan came and sat beside me. He looked me in the eyes,

"John, is this what you really want?"

I pointed to the encyclopedia volumes still lying open and strewn across the floor,

"Take a look at that, Alan," I said, "If you were my age and given the choice of dishing out fuses and screws for the rest of your life or getting a proper job and traveling the world, what would you do?"

Alan thought for a moment, his eyes alternating between my face and the books. Finally he said,

"Right, when you fill in the forms don't put Wardlow. From now on you are John Skull and any criminal check will come up clean. I'll get your name changed by deed poll. And don't worry about your mother, I'll make sure she signs the consent forms. I think you'll make a great sailor, mate."

With that, he ruffled my hair and left me with my thoughts. These thoughts were a confused jumble of guilt and desire. Guilt because my mother clearly wanted me to stay, but the desire to leave was just too strong. I really appreciated what Alan had done by bringing the whole family back together, but I really did not feel a strong sense of being wanted or needed. The truth was that Alan was extremely busy building a successful career and I really did not feel too connected to my mother. After all, when I was young child she wasn't there and when she did occasionally return, it caused more trouble, violence and unhappiness in my already crappy childhood. Also, I was 16-years old and it was time to start making my own way in the world. Welcome, John Skull!

The next morning, I called Wilf and told him that I'd fallen off my moped, sprained my wrist and couldn't come to work. He was not happy,

"Swollen wrist, swollen wrist? I've only got one fucking hand and I'm here!"

I searched the Yellow Pages and discovered that the nearest navy recruiting office was in Dorchester, the County town of Dorset and

If You Can't Take a Joke…

about 30 miles west of Ferndown. I decided to go directly there and pick up some brochures and as much information as I could before starting the application process. I had only ever ridden my moped the two or so miles to and from work, but did not anticipate a problem with a 60 mile round trip. I did the maths. Sixty miles at 30 miles per hour equals two hours, right? Wrong. As I mentioned previously, my faithful Batavus could reach 30 miles per hour downhill, with the wind behind me. Unfortunately, the A31 and A35 to Dorchester is not downhill and the prevailing wind is from the west. It rained too. After half an hour and about eight miles my face was red raw from the cold October wind and rain, my feet were numb from the constant vibration from the foot pegs and my arse was severely chafed by the narrow seat. I was riding along the main road to the west of England and about once a minute, I was overtaken by large trucks, showered by gallons of dirty spray and knocked sideways by the slipstream. It was a miserable, uncomfortable and dangerous trip, but I could not stop. I was on a mission. At about 2.00pm that afternoon, I finally opened the door to the recruiting office. The Chief Petty Officer looked up and saw a bedraggled youth dripping dirty water and walking towards him with his feet so far apart he looked like a giraffe at feeding time. I am sure that with my arrival he relaxed, secure in the knowledge that the British Empire's defence was about to receive a much needed boost. Or not. Within a couple of minutes, he was sitting behind his desk while I sat opposite, both hands wrapped around a mug of steaming, sweet tea. I explained to him that I had come to pick up some brochures and forms about joining up and to find out about the procedures. I tried to sound confident and older than my sixteen years, but failed,

"Have you spoken with your parents about this?"

I told him that my father had been a career soldier and that both my parents were very keen for me to follow his footsteps into the Armed Forces. I thought it wise not to mention that I was no longer living with my father and if asked, he would probably say that the Queen would probably be better off without me. The Chief Petty Officer explained that the process was quite straightforward and that all I had to do was take some tests and depending on how well I did, he would recommend what career path would be best for me. I had not thought about what I would do in the navy at all and when he told me the occupations on offer, I thought that he had suddenly started speaking in tongues.

"Well, you could be a stoker, greenie, dabto, wafu, jack dusty, deck ape or a bunting tosser."

He laughed as my eyes glazed over,

"Don't worry, son, you'll soon find out that we have a different language in the navy. What I said was that you could be a mechanical engineer, a radar plotter, work with helicopters, a storeman, a seaman or a tactical communications rating. All depends on how you do in the tests. Let us get them done now, as you are already here shall we? No point in having to do that trip again is there?"

Nervously, I nodded. I really had not expected to do any tests that day. All I really wanted was some more information. I had no experience of doing tests since I passed my eleven-plus five years previously and did not know what to expect. I didn't know if I was even smart enough. My schooling had been intermittent, but I must have learned something. I knew the difference between a clarinet and an oboe. I was good at doing sums in my head. My spelling and, to a lesser degree my grammar, were passable and I knew that the Battle of Trafalgar had taken place on 21st October 1805. Okay, I had only known that for less than a day, but I still knew it. How do I know this stuff? Was it from school, or the long hours reading anything I could lay my hands on at the back of the classroom in Rathgael? In any case, a few minutes later I was seated in a training room behind the front office with a stack of test papers in front of me. As I worked my way through the papers, my confidence grew. Simple maths and comprehension tests, followed by an IQ test where you had to complete the next two numbers in the sequence or know that SHOES are to FEET as GLOVES are to HANDS. It became quickly apparent that to be a wafu or dabto did not require any knowledge of brain science or rocket surgery. The reality was that the tests were simply designed to determine that you had the ability to read and understand training materials and that your level of comprehension was suffice to obey simple verbal instructions like,

"Polish those shoes until I can see my face in them!"

The Chief took my papers away and marked them. Back at his desk, he enthusiastically informed me that I had done so well in the tests that I could join as a radio operator, which would be much better than painting decks or humping stores, wouldn't it? At his direction, I started completing the application forms then and there. It was funny writing 'Skull' in the surname box for the first time, but I could not risk not being allowed to join because of my previous dishonesty. Much better to lie. After I signed the last form, the Chief held out his hand,

"Welcome to the Royal Navy, son."

I took his hand, "Is that it, then?"

The Chief told me that that indeed was it and that all I had to do was return the consent form signed by my parents and they would let me know when and where to join. I do not remember the moped ride home, but with the wind now behind me and my thoughts racing ahead, I am sure it was much easier. Alan and my mother were sitting at the dining room table as I burst through the door. As I approached them, Alan gave me a conspiratorial wink,

"How'd it go, John?"

I think that the look on my face provided an answer enough and I produced the consent forms and hesitantly pushed them towards my mother. The Chief had helped by highlighting the correct section and mum quickly read the relevant paragraph, then signed it. She looked a little sad, so rather than display the joy I was feeling inside, I simply said,

"Thanks, mum."

Within two weeks, I had returned the forms to Dorchester and received a reply directing that I should report for duty at HMS Ganges on 18th February 1975. I do not know if Alan ever did change my name legally, but I was now John Skull. With my new name and new career ahead of me, I also felt a new confidence. Look out world.

Part II

Chapter 22 – Navy Days

During the early afternoon of 18th February 1975, I was sitting on Platform 3 at Liverpool Street Station in London. Having spent a year in Rathgael being tied to routine and timetables, I was a stickler for being at the right place at the right time, so had arrived early. It was a Tuesday, so there weren't too many people lingering at the platform. My joining instructions had included rail warrants to get me to Ipswich and also comprehensive instructions as to what I should bring with me. Again, like Rathgael, the civilian clothes that I was travelling in would be taken from me upon arrival at HMS Ganges and I wouldn't see them until after the six week basic training period. I was to bring seven pairs of underpants, two pairs of pyjamas, two towels, a toothbrush, toothpaste, deodorant, soap, shampoo and a comb, all of which should be carried in one small bag. That was it. No socks, vests, books, writing materials, radios, watches, jewelry, photos, sunglasses or anything that would mark me out as an individual. As I sat there with my bag on my lap and a brown paper bag with some sandwiches and lemonade for the trip, I noticed a number of other young men around the platform with their single bag and looks of concern and doubt, mingled with excitement and hope. I wondered if I looked like that. The public address system burst into life with a long announcement and, in accordance with British Rail customs of that era, everyone looked around for a British Rail employee to interpret the feedback and echoes into a message that normal folk could understand. As one battle-weary train guard moved along the platform answering the same question time and time again, he left behind him a trail of chins dropping disappointedly onto chests. The train, in accordance with British Rail customs of that era, was delayed and would depart an hour later than the scheduled time. It was a chilly February afternoon, so everyone headed to the station cafe for a hot drink. I joined the queue for a cup of tea, which was eventually served in a polystyrene cup and then I joined the queue for sugar. A tea and coffee stained bag of Tate & Lyle sugar and one single teaspoon, remarkably with a hole drilled in the handle and chained to the table, were the cause of the queuing. The train finally arrived and all the young men with rail warrants, rather than tickets, were herded to the front carriage which had a large "HMS GANGES ONLY" poster in the window. There were just over a dozen recruits in this group, all around my age, and we chose our seats. Some clustered together and others, like me, found a quiet seat away from the crowd. I was still nervous about my Belfast accent and didn't want to become the focus of attention or worse. As I listened to the banter of the group, I detected accents from all over Great Britain, including Birmingham, Manchester and a couple who'd even traveled down from Scotland. The train had been delayed due to track works and the trip which normally took around ninety minutes dragged on for around three hours. I was getting pretty peckish, but resisted the temptation to open my sandwich bag, as I wasn't sure when I'd eat again so decided to keep them as 'emergency rations'. I just stared out of the window

If You Can't Take a Joke...

as London disappeared behind us and nodded on and off occasionally, relaxed by the clackety-clack and gentle swaying of the train. We finally pulled into Ipswich just after six o'clock to a cheer from many of the passengers. As I emerged from the front of the station, I took my sandwiches out of my bag as by this time I was ravenous. But before I could start eating, I was almost blinded by the shiniest Ford Transit Van I'd ever seen. 'ROYAL NAVY' was proudly emblazoned in blue along the side of the vehicle in sharp contrast to the dazzling white of the bodywork. Somewhat disappointed, I put the sarnies bag in my bag. The tyres of the van looked like they had been spit and polished and the chrome sparkled like diamonds as beading drops of rain dripped off like escaping spirit level bubbles. From behind it emerged an even shinier sailor. Tall, square of jaw and handsome, the creases of his uniform looked like they could slice bread.

"Right," he shouted above the wind and rain, "HMS Ganges boys over here and fall in one behind the other twice!"

After some confusion, it appeared that this meant we should line up in three rows. He conducted a roll call and, apparently satisfied that all sixteen recruits he was expecting were present and correct, ordered,

"Right, you scrotes, get in the van." I assumed that the first rank one gains as a member of the RN was Scrote. Given that I was only 16, I was probably only a Junior Scrote Second Class!

During quite a long career in the Royal Navy, I was to make a few mistakes. I never expected to make my first quite so quickly. As I was

If You Can't Take a Joke…

about to climb into the Transit, a small notice caught my eye. "MAX PASS 12". I turned to the shiny sailor and , trying to be helpful, said,

"Excuse me, Sir, I think there are 16 of us, but it says only 12 can be carried at one time in the van."

He didn't miss a beat,

"Don't call me 'Sir'…I work for a fucking living! Okay, everybody out. Fall in. C'mon move it!"

We duly fell in one behind the other twice. Our escort addressed me directly,

"What's your name?"

"John."

His voice increased in volume,

"Do I look like I need another friend? I don't care what your fucking mother calls you! What is your last name?"

"Oh, sorry…. It's Skull, John Skull," I mumbled, hating being the focus of attention.

Shiny Sailor addressed the rest of the group, more calmly,

"Mr. Skull here has pointed out, quite correctly as it happens, that this vehicle is only licenced to carry 12 passengers so this means that I'll have to make two trips to Ganges. It is now nearly 6.30pm and it takes about half an hour to get to Ganges, so by the time I get back for the second group, it'll be 7.30pm."

I could feel a degree of resentment towards me building up from the rest of the group, but worse was to come. Just as it appeared that my new friend had finished, he turned to the group once more,

"Oh," he said, as if struck by an afterthought, "One more thing. The galley closes at 7.00pm, so only the first group will be able to have dinner."

He paused, then looked me directly in the eyes,

"Mr. Skull, I'll let you decide who goes on the first trip and who stays behind with you."

During the train journey, I had observed only some slightly nervous and excited young men about to embark on an adventure, but as I turned to look at them now I saw something else. They looked cold, wet, angry....and hungry. Twelve could go on the first trip so I had to pick three to stay behind with me. I picked the smallest. We watched despondently as the shiny Ford Transit headed off towards Ganges and a hot meal. We moved back to the waiting room and sat down to await the return of our transport, me alone on a bench and the others sitting directly opposite, just staring at me. I remember glancing up at the timetable and had there been another train returning to London I have no doubt I would have boarded it. One of them stood up and stopped directly in front of me. I tensed myself for the punch that was undoubtedly coming my way, but he simply reached down and took my brown paper bag. They ate my sandwiches.

Chapter 23 – HMS GANGES

In the mid-1800s the Royal Navy was becoming increasingly technical and professional. It was decided that instead of young men being thrust into the rough and tough world of life at sea to carry out 'on the job training', there should be ships adapted purely for a training role. One of these was the 84-gun ship of the line, HMS Ganges. Although refitted for training, with accommodation for up to 500 boys, she did not have an auspicious start as a training vessel. Her first Commanding Officer and First Lieutenant were removed from the ship after allegations of mistreatment. Under Commander F.W. Wilson, her new Commanding Officer, she flourished and was based in Cornwall for some years before eventually arriving in Shotley, Ipswich. There she became an integral part of the Royal Naval Training Establishment Shotley. In 1906 HMS Ganges was renamed and moved on to other duties, but her name and training pedigree were both recognized and in 1927 when the training establishment at Shotley was rebuild, it was named HMS Ganges. The original ship of the line was broken up in 1930, but the Captain's cabin was used in the construction of the art-deco Burgh Island luxury hotel in Devon. The HMS Ganges I found myself in was anything but luxurious. Upon our late arrival, we were herded into an area called the Long Covered Way, which consisted of a number of large dormitories. I was allocated to Resolution Division and suddenly everything reminded me of Rathgael Reception block. Although these buildings were built during the Victorian era, everything about the dormitories was clean, tidy and totally squared away, just like Shiny Sailor and his Transit van. There were about forty beds in the dormitory and after a long day, we were soon all safely tucked up in our beds. Young men were trying to get to know each other and pretending to be tough, but once the lights went out at 10 o'clock sharp, I could hear more than one lonely young man sobbing, probably for his mother. Just like Rathgael.

The following morning we were rudely awakened at 6 o'clock by shouting and clanging of bin lids,

"Hands off cocks and on your socks, ladies. Let's be fucking having you! Standby your beds, you shower of shit," shouted yet another impossibly immaculate sailor.

We crawled out of our warm beds and stood in the chilly messdeck at what we thought was attention.

"Chins up, chests out! If you ain't got a fucking chest yet, you soon will. Right, I want you fell in outside in 30 minutes ready for breakfast. Before then you'll all have shat, shaved, showered and shampooed. Now, MOVE IT!"

I wasn't entirely convinced that all this shouting was necessary, but given my experience of the previous night, I kept my reservations to myself and joined the hive of activity that was morning ablutions. In half an hour, we were lined up outside the Resolution mess-deck ready to be marched to breakfast. By now, our new-entry ranks had swollen to about 60, as we were joined by those who arrived by bus and train from different stations. We were still in our civilian clothes and looked more like a school outing than a fighting force. This being the mid-70s, many of us wore our hair past our collars in the style of the

If You Can't Take a Joke...

day. Flares, flowery shirts and the odd pair of platform shoes made their way slowly to the dining hall and we were greeted by howls of laughter and screams of,

"Nozzers!"

"Sprogs!"

"Got a boyfriend, darlin'?"

"Wankers!"

I was soon to find out that these were basically expressions of relief from veterans of two weeks' service, simply overjoyed that they had moved off the bottom of the food chain. It was clear that some of my fellow recruits were finding all this very challenging, but having already spent years in institutions I took it easily in my stride. There is a maxim in the Royal Navy that the navy cook's course is the hardest, because no-one has successfully completed it! All the ingredients for a hearty breakfast were there, including bacon, eggs, beans, sausages, bread and tea - coffee was exclusively for the RAF! Everything lay on metal trays, looking more like an autopsy than breakfast. The bacon resembled slices of lung with blubbery tumours of fat, while the eggs were fried to within an inch of ice hockey puck consistency. Having said that, I had not eaten for nearly 24 hours and devoured the lot. After breakfast, we were marched to the establishment barber shop. It reminded me of a chicken processing plant that I'd seen recently on television, with fine feathered birds going in one end and coming out the other ready for the oven. Inside the shop four barbers were lined up behind their chairs, just waiting for their victims. We all knew, of course, that this moment would come, but some of the faces of the young recruits bore expressions of, if not terror, at least severe apprehension. There were no scissors to be seen, but each of the barbers wielded a heavy pair of electric clippers and I half expected that we'd be upended, gripped between the knees of the barbers and shorn like sheep. My immediate reaction after having my fair, possibly strawberry blonde and definitely not ginger locks fall around my feet like the feathers of a hastily plucked duck, was how cold it felt around my neck and ears – February in Ipswich!

Within minutes we were once more lined up in ranks, split into classes of around twenty recruits and marched to the supply department for the issue of our uniforms and personal kit. As with breakfast and the barber shop, issue of clothing and equipment were carried out with the speed and efficiency of a factory production line. And this particular production line didn't stop for a very long time. Everything I would need for my entire naval career was dumped into a large beige canvas kitbag. Boots, shoes, plimsolls, working uniforms, ceremonial uniforms, tropical uniforms, beret, hats (lids), raincoat (burberry), windjacket (windy-burb), knife, lanyard, a mysterious roll of white ribbon, black inkpad, white inkpad, name stamp, sewing kits and shoe-brushes. We left the storeroom and piled our now bulging kitbags onto a trolley and were marched back to our messdeck in the Long Covered Way. We dumped our kit beside our beds and were joined by Petty Officer Archibald, our instructor for basic training, and his assistant, Leading Seaman Cook. PO Archibald had us gather around in a group. Beside him was a column of stacked books which

If You Can't Take a Joke…

reached his waist. He leaned on the books as he started his welcoming address in a rasping voice straight out of a 1950s war movie,

"You are now part of Resolution Division, a division of which I am proud. If you do anything to bring the Resolution name into disrepute, I will fuck you up. For the next six weeks, I will be your instructor, mentor and only family that matters. Your mummies and daddies aren't here, so you'll come to me if you are sick, sad, sore or scared."

He looked around at his new children, paused for effect and then soberly indicated the pile of books,

"These books are the Queen's Regulations for the Royal Navy. There are too many rules in there for you to memorise, so I've condensed the QRRNs for you."

From his pocket he removed a small square of folded paper, carefully opened it and cleared his throat,

"Number one. No fucking poofters. Number two. Do what you're fucking told. Number three. There is no fucking number three. All you need is the first two rules. Any questions. No? Good!"

Given my previous experience concerning the passenger capacity of the Transit van, I thought it best to hold my tongue. No-one else had questions either, so PO Archibald continued,

"For the rest of the day, you'll be working on your kit, so that the next time I see you I'll be looking at sailors and not the sad bunch of fucking hippies and weirdos I see before me now."

He called his assistant alongside him with a nod of his head,

If You Can't Take a Joke...

"This fine example of the British fighting sailor is my right-hand man, Leading Seaman Cook. You can call him Leading Seaman Cook, Leader or Hookie. He'll be looking after you for the rest of the day and helping you get your kit sorted. Welcome to the Royal Navy."

PO Archibald turned on his heel and walked smartly from the messdeck. Leading Seaman Cook told us to empty our kitbags onto our beds and stow all footwear at the bottom of our lockers and then he'd show us what to do after that. We followed Rule number two. It was shortly after this that LS Cook punched me.

I had wanted to ask him a question. Most people were aware that the army indicates ranks by the number of stripes worn on the arm – one for lance-corporal, two for corporal and three for sergeant. Most people, including me, didn't know the navy system. I didn't know, for example, that the rank badge for a Leading Seaman was an anchor, or 'hook' as it is known in the navy. So when PO Archibald had informed us that one of the options for addressing LS Cook was Hookie, I thought he was using the nickname Cookie. As Leading Seaman Cook, alias Leader or Hookie passed by my bed, I said,

"Excuse me, Cookie…."

LS Cook swung around, dropped me with a right hook and stood over me,

"It's Hookie, you cunt, Hookie!"

Welcome to the Royal Navy indeed.

Chapter 24 – Learning the Ropes

During the next few weeks, we actually did become more like the fighting men England required, but not before we had mastered some proper manly tasks. We were taught how to wash our clothes, how to iron them and how to repair them. The first sewing challenge involved the mysterious roll of white ribbon we were issued on the first day. This ribbon was cut into strips, stamped with 'J.R.SKULL' and sewn onto shirts. Everything else was stamped – blue items with white dye and white items with black. Remembering that all the training we would undertake over the next few months was aimed at preparing us for life at sea, everything we did was geared to working aboard a ship. Our lockers at HMS GANGES were the same size and design as those on the ships and everything had to fit inside. All items of clothing were ironed and then folded to exactly the size of Volume IV of the Seamanship Manual. We had our entire kit mustered every week, laid out on our beds according to the picture in the manual and only perfection was acceptable. Failure to pass the inspection was subtly indicated by one's bed, mattress and entire kit, being upturned and this meant it all had to be done again on Saturday morning. I don't think I missed a Saturday morning re-muster, given that I was absolutely hopeless at ironing and anything to do with uniforms. It might have been my size, my shape or just my physical demeanour, but if I'd been dressed in a tailor-made suit from Savile Row I'd still looked like a bag of potatoes with a head. Shoes and boots had to be spit-polished to a mirror-like finish, but that was another skill that I never mastered and had to pay someone else to do.

The harshness of the training regime nearly forty years ago would not be acceptable today. There were no group hugs, no beanbag group sessions, no counseling, no sick notes, no molly-coddling and no excuses. You did what you were told to do, how you were told to do it, when to do it and without question. It was all about discipline and blind obedience. One of the best methods of instilling this mantra into our developing minds was drill practice. Hours and hours of marching up and down the parade ground in freezing February and March, with no allowance made for weather or common sense. Left, right, left, right, about turn, squad halt, forms threes, eyes right, stand at ease, stand easy. Of course, marching is simply walking, but I was amazed at how many people couldn't quite do it. We'd line up, one behind the other twice of course, at the beginning of drill practice. Before we were allowed to move, the morning inspection would be conducted by Petty Officer Archibald. He would stand in front of each of us in turn and ensure that our creases could cut diamonds and that the reflection from our boots could be seen from space. At our first inspection, he stopped in front of each recruit and had the same conversation,

"Name?"

"Smith, Sir?"

"Don't call me 'sir', I fucking work for a living!"

"Sorry, sir..... I mean PO. My name is Smith, PO."

If You Can't Take a Joke…

"Right. Everyone in the navy 'as a nickname and Smiths are called Smudge."

The Petty Officer would move along to the next victim,

"Name?"

"Collins, PO."

"Right, you're Jumper Collins from now on. All Collins' in the navy are called Jumper."

And so our education would continue with Bungy Edwards (and Williams), Knocker White, Buster Brown, Skippy Jump, Tiny Little, Fanny Adams, Bagsy Baker and Dinger Bell. If, like me, you had an uncommon name then a physical or geographical nickname would be applied, so for the next 15 years I was known as Paddy Skull, joining the ranks of Jocks, Taffs, Brummies, Scouses and Geordies. It wasn't as bad as some, as you're about to discover. Petty Archibald continued the inspection and stood in front of the next recruit,

"Name?"

"Doyle-Davidson, PO," replied Doyle-Davidson in a distinctly posh accent.

Archibald appeared somewhat taken aback,

"Are you in the wrong fucking line, son?"

"I don't think so, PO."

"Hmmmm, Doyle-Davidson. Don't think we've had one of those before….let me think….. Doyle hyphen Davidson…. D hypen D….got it! Dil-Do is your new name!"

At the end of the parade ground there was a large rubbish skip and whenever one of the recruits made a mistake during drill practice, he would be made to run around the parade ground with his rifle above his head and then climb into the skip. When his name was called by the drill instructor, the recruit was required to stick his head above the rim of the skip, shout his name and declare that he was gash – rubbish, in naval parlance. Poor Doyle-Davidson was useless at marching and would regularly be seen popping his head out of the skip,

"I'M DILDO AND I'M RUBBISH!"

During another morning parade ground inspection, I fell foul of the foul Petty Officer Archibald.

"Smith, did you shave this morning?"

"Yes, PO."

"WELL USE A FUCKING RAZOR NEXT TIME!"

"Baker, did you shave this morning?"

"Yes, PO."

"SHAVE CLOSER NEXT TIME!"

"Skull, did you shave this morning?"

"Yes, PO."

"WHY?"

Over the next few weeks the vigorous adherence to timetables and orders, coupled with strenuous physical activity slowly turned our ragbag intake into the makings of sailors. The academic work was not overly challenging, however delving into a thousand years of naval history brought me an understanding of the fierce pride exhibited by the staff at HMS Ganges. After the Transit van and 'Cookie' incidents, I had quickly learned the value of keeping a low profile and did well on any tests that were taken and even started to look like a proper sailor, even if I was a little creased around the edges. Time was also set aside for the new recruits to write letters home. As I stared at the blank page in front of me, I could not think of a single word to write. I was not homesick, nor did I have any letters from home to provide inspiration. Clearly, I was not missed and I was fine with that.

Chapter 25 – The Run Ashore

After six weeks, we were allowed our first 'run ashore'. This is the term used for any leave from either ship or shore establishment. One stipulation was that we had to go ashore in uniform, which had its inherent risks. The local lads resented the navy boys, as there was a perception that we only went ashore to take their women. It was true that whilst many of the young men in the area were unemployed, broke or both, we had been locked up in Ganges for six weeks with nothing to spend our money on and this may have made us slightly more attractive to the young ladies. The nearest place for us to enjoy a night out was across the river in Harwich. As always, nothing could be done without a prior inspection so about ten of us lined up just inside the main gate of HMS Ganges and were inspected by the Duty Petty Officer. Fortunately it was a cold evening and the inspection was just a cursory glance to ensure that we were not likely to bring the Royal Navy into disrepute. Being only sixteen years old and a junior, my leave expired at midnight and woe betide any juniors who were 'adrift' – late back. As we walked out of the gates of HMS Ganges for the first time in six weeks, there was a high degree of self-consciousness as we strutted down the street in our immaculate uniforms. Some of the older recruits looked the part, but I felt that I more resembled a schoolboy playing dress-up than a salty seadog and was simply trying to mimic the actions and attitude of the grown-ups. After a short, choppy ferry ride across the brown and murky Stour River we found ourselves standing on the jetty in Harwich. The more experienced

If You Can't Take a Joke...

men took on the appearance of a mob of meerkats as they sniffed the air and scanned the horizon for the nearest watering hole. It was a dark and dismal April evening, but a few paces up King's Quay Street, the warm orange glow of The Globe pub beckoned us. The pace increased, as did the smacking of lips and uplifting of spirits. Soon we were seated comfortably around a couple of tables in the bar. I couldn't mention it to the others, but this was my first time in a pub, with the exception of a couple of family pub lunches. A warm fire glowed in the corner and a couple of old-timers supped their pints as they warmed themselves. Shadows formed by the flames danced across the wooden paneling up to the yellow nicotine stained anaglypta wallpaper and the smell of stale cigarettes, stale beer and fire smoke added to the authentic pub experience. All that was missing was a pint of frothing ale in front of me. Being only sixteen years old, it was not legal for me to drink. I watched as the rest of the guys returned in small groups or individually from the bar, licking away fresh froth moustaches from their top lips. I approached the bar, looking as old and tough as I could and caught the barman's eye. He stopped in front of me,

"Beer, please mate", I squeaked.

"What sort?"

"Lager?"

"Which one?"

"Ehm.... ", I glanced at the taps, "Worthington E, please."

"That's not lager."

"What is it, then?"

"Oh, for fuck's sake, son. I know you're not eighteen, but I reckon if you are old enough to serve your country, you're old enough to drink in my pub, but you're going to have to help me out here. Now, why don't you fuck off back to your mates for a minute, sort out what you'd like and then come back to the bar, like a man, and tell me what you fucking want!"

I felt my face burning as I returned to my seat. Taff Williams, one of my course mates asked,

"No drink, Paddy?"

"Nah, not sure what I want. What are you having?" I answered.

"Thanks very much, I'll have another pint!" he laughed, draining the rest of his drink.

Everyone laughed good naturedly. I was still confused, but it suddenly dawned on me that 'What are you having?' is pubspeak for buying someone a drink. I joined in the laughter,

"All right, Taff. What are you drinking?"

"Cheers, Paddy, I'll have a pint of lager." He said unhelpfully.

"Okay, which one?"

"Stella."

The landlord saw me approach his bar for the second time.

"Hello, mate, what can I get for you?" he asked cheerfully, as if he'd never seen me before.

"Coupla pints of Stella, please?"

"Coming up."

He put the pints in front of me and as he handed me my change, he leaned conspiratorially towards me and whispered,

If You Can't Take a Joke...

"See, son? Nothing to worry about!"

Before I knew it, I was one of the boys. Good natured barracking, the odd risqué joke, exaggerated recollections of our recent experiences and mutual backslapping all combined to draw us closer together. The heat from the fire warmed me on the outside and the lager warmed the inside.

We had been amongst the first people in the bar, but as the evening drew on, the pub became more crowded and the volume increased as everyone tried to be heard above the drone of pub chatter. The quick beer after work crowd was slowly drifting off, to be replaced with those who were out for the evening. Suited-and-tied office workers and overalled-and-workbooted labourers shuffled off home and the miniskirted-and-stilettoed girls and flared-and-platformed boys came out to play. This was the mid-70s and 'glam-rock' was at its height – androgynous hairstyles and clothing the norm. More than once, I'd oggled shamelessly at the back of a head with long blonde flowing locks falling over an attractive lilac paisley blouse, only to be slammed back to reality when the blonde turned out to have a healthy ginger moustache. The table next to ours was suddenly occupied by four girls, getting ready for a big night out. It was readily apparent that they had started imbibing before they got to the bar and their giggling and laughter, coupled with a rather wonderful smell, soon drew the attention of the boys at our table. Paul 'Jack' Russell, a twenty year-old recruit from London was, in naval jargon, a fanny-rat. Apparently fueled solely by pheromones and testosterone, Paul did a round-robin of the girls' table, trying and failing with a series of dreadful pickup lines,

"Congratulations! You have just been voted "Most Beautiful Girl In This Room" and the grand prize is a night with me!"

"I wonder what our children will look like!"

And the ever popular,

"This face leaves at eleven – be on it!"

Ungracious in defeat, Paul returned to our table,

"Obviously all fucking lesbians!"

During Paul's tour of the ladies' table, I had caught the eye of one particular girl at the table and we exchanged shy smiles. I noticed that she didn't have a drink, so fortified by around three pints of Stella and feeling courageous, I approached her table. I must have been a bit nervous, as I wobbled slightly before saying,

"Hi, I'm Paddy. I was just getting another drink and wondered if you'd like one?"

"Lovely," she smiled, "A Bacardi and Black, please."

Of course, I'd never heard of Bacardi and Black and was curious enough to forego my next pint of Stella to try this new drink. I returned to the bar once again, and asked confidently,

"Two pints of Bacardi and Black, please."

My new found friend, the landlord replied,

"They don't come in pints."

"Two half pints?"

"Nope"

"Two bottles of Bacardi and Black?"

"Not even close, sailor."

"Ok, can I have two drinks of Bacardi and Black, please?"

"Certainly, sir. Tall or short?"

Oh for fuck's sake. I had no idea what he was talking about, so guessed,

"Long, please."

Finally, he placed two long glasses, of course, of a dark purple concoction on the bar in front of me, with his now familiar wink, and took my proffered pound note. As he returned my change, he leaned over the bar towards me,

"Her name's Jean, mate, and she's known a lot of sailors, if you get my drift."

One more wink and he turned to play twenty questions with another novice drinker. Despite racking my now slightly addled brain, I didn't get his drift at all. It was blatantly obvious, to me at least, that as she lived near the closest bar to HMS Ganges it was blatantly obvious that she would know a lot of sailors. While I was at the bar, Jean, if indeed that was her name, had squeezed another chair beside her and invited me to join her, so I sat down. I place her drink in front of her,

"Here you go…… Jean, isn't it?"

"Yes, how did you know?"

"Oh, the landlord saw me talking to you and told me."

"What else did he tell you?"

"Nothing, that was it."

"Okay, but if he says anything, don't believe him, 'cos he's a lying twat."

I was slightly shocked at the change in tone, but decided to change the subject. This was just about the longest conversation I'd ever had with a girl, so I was desperate to sound mature and worldly,

"Bacardi and Black, eh? Quite exotic for Harwich, isn't it?"

She gave me a quizzical look – a look with which I was to become increasingly familiar from females.

"Nah, I drink it a lot. Beer makes me want to piss all the time."

She lifted her glass and held it towards me,

"Cheers then, Paddy."

I dutifully clinked her glass with mine and we each took a sip. Bacardi and black, as it turns out, is white Bacardi Rum, ice and blackcurrant cordial. The first sip coated my entire mouth with a sickly sweet syrup and I'm not sure if the head-spin I felt was alcohol or a sugar rush. Jean wasn't much of a sipper, though, and in two gulps her glass was empty. She wiped her new purple moustache from her top lip and looked at me,

"I'd get you one, but I'm skint, Paddy."

As we sat together talking, I was very conscious of the fact that her thigh was rubbing against mine and no matter how often I moved to give her a bit more room, our thighs would end up touching again. I liked it. I was worried that she'd go, if she didn't have a drink, so I offered,

"That's okay, I was just going back to the bar anyway, so I'll get you one."

After ordering the next round of drinks, apparently correctly as there were no supplementary questions from the winker behind the bar, I looked around at Jean as I waited for them to arrive. I may have been examining her through purple-tinted glasses, but I thought she was adorable. Not pretty in the conventional sense, nor particularly slim, for that matter. Her hair was blonde, mainly at the ends and her face was wrinkle free, possibly because of the slight chubbiness of her features. In this glam-rock era, I didn't think her outfit was overly outrageous, but the amount of ample cleavage on show was possibly a little over the top. I didn't know what you've already guessed about Jean, but this was my first night in a pub, my first serious drinking and my first possibility of getting off with a girl, so don't judge me! Anyway, as I made my way back to my seat, Taffy shouted from across the bar,

"Go on, Paddy, my son!"

The rest of my mates laughed loudly and cheered me on, so I smiled and made my way back to my table, where I saw Jean glance at her watch with a frown. Again, I squeezed in beside her,

"You got to be somewhere, Jean?"

Another one of her quizzical looks and,

"No, but we should probably go somewhere a bit quieter, don't you think?"

I hadn't actually been thinking that and, in fact, with a number of pints and a couple of Bacardi's in me, I wasn't thinking too much at all. She picked up her drink, clinked my glass and emptied hers without the need for the swallow reflex.

If You Can't Take a Joke...

"C'mon, let's go!"

I tried to gulp down the rest of my drink, but Jean had grabbed my hand and was practically dragging me from the pub. I could hear the cheers from my mates as the pub door closed behind me and we were blasted by the cold evening air.

"Slow down, Jean! Where are we going anyway?"

At this point, I was as close to snogging a girl as I'd ever been and was desperate not to spoil the mood, so I tried hard to think of something devastatingly romantic to say. I was drunk, but I still managed to come up with,

"Jean, there's no need to rush. After all, we've got the rest of our lives!"

Devastating, I know. I took half a pace back and waited for her to envelope me in her arms and with a tear in her eye, kiss me passionately. She didn't.

"What the fuck are you talking about? I've got a regular in half-an-hour, so I'll have to do you in the alley behind the pub. It's fucking freezing, so I'm not taking anything off. Blow job or nothing, Paddy. Five quid."

Looking back, I'm slightly embarrassed at how long it took for me to grasp the reality of my situation, but I was young, naive and had spent much of my youth in male only environments. I knew what a blow job was, but I hadn't even kissed a girl before, so I thought that this was too large a step on the sexual continuum for one so young. Well, that and the fact that I didn't have five quid left after buying her bloody drinks all night. I don't think I even responded to her offer, unless you consider turning around and legging it as quickly as my slightly wobbly pins would take me back to the ferry point as any sort of response.

Chapter 26 – HMS MERCURY – Communicators Alma Mater

With our basic training now successfully completed, the boys from Resolution went our separate ways. The Radio Operators to HMS Mercury, the Stokers to HMS Sultan, the Electrical Mechanics to HMS Collingwood and the Radar, Sonar and other seaman ratings to HMS Dryad – all shore establishments in Hampshire. The Stores and Secretariat ratings including Writers, Stores Assistants, Stewards and Cooks, went off to HMS Pembroke, near Chatham Dockyard in Kent.

The shore establishment to which I was drafted, HMS Mercury, was at least the nineteenth use of that name, with the previous seventeen being ships – the first a 6-gun galley launched in 1592. My HMS Mercury was situated around 12 miles north of Portsmouth Naval Base and Dockyard. The signaling school was established at Leydene House in August 1941 at the height of World War II under the command of Captain Gerald Warner. It went on to house not only the communications school, but later became the Navigators faculty of the School of Maritime Operations and also the home of the Special Communications Unit Leydene. Between April 1975 and April 1996 I would attend all three faculties.

In April 1975, however, I had no idea what the next 21 days entailed let alone the next 21 years.

So after a short and entirely uneventful leave break at home in Ferndown, it was a train trip to Petersfield and yet another minibus up the hill to HMS Mercury. Although still very junior trainees, there was

If You Can't Take a Joke...

a little let up in the spit-and-shine bullshit suffered at Ganges, but make no mistake, we were still the lowest of the low – in the marine life pecking order, our position was somewhere between krill and amoeba. We formed part of Kelly Squadron, named after the World War II destroyer HMS Kelly. This famous ship was captained by the most famous modern Royal Navy Communicator, Lord Louis Mountbatten, who was a frequent visitor to HMS Mercury. I recall that at one point we were required to memorise his full title - Admiral of the Fleet Louis Francis Albert Victor Nicholas Mountbatten, 1st Earl Mountbatten of Burma, KG, GCB, OM, GCSI, GCIE, GCVO, DSO, PC, FRS.

Being ignored by Lord Louis as he chats to the recruit next to me

If You Can't Take a Joke...

Our accommodation improved significantly and we were allocated to six-man messes in the Junior Ratings blocks along Crescent Road. I was in Howe Block and this was to be my home for the next six months.

Just as we were congratulating ourselves on our new status, we were informed that first thing the next morning we were to undergo a full kit muster. I was still pretty useless at washing, ironing, sewing and polishing, so inevitably had to 're-scrub' nearly every kit muster. I remember one kit muster in particular. All our kit was either black, blue or white and each piece of kit had to be stamped with our name – white ink on blue/black kit and black ink on white kit. Not only that, but for the kit muster, all the kit had to be folded in such a way that the name was on display. I think it was my second muster at Mercury and I was so late and flustered that I forgot that particular step, so although my kit was very neatly 'squared away' on my bunk, none of it had my name showing. We had to formally present our kit to our Divisional Officer, Fleet Chief Communications Yeoman (FCCY) Chris Bracey,

"JRO Skull reporting, Sir. Kit ready for inspection."

FCCY Bracey approached my bunk and inspected my kit. A puzzled look appeared on his face,

"Whose kit is this?"

"Mine, Sir." I replied.

"How do I know that? It could be stolen!" He turned to the Duty Petty Officer,

"PO, do you know whose kit this is?"

If You Can't Take a Joke…

"No idea, Sir. No names on it….could be stolen!"

Of course, I realised immediately the error of my ways, but too late.

The PO stepped forward,

"Excuse me, Sir, I may have a solution."

"Happy to hear it PO. Carry on."

At this, the Duty Petty Officer stood beside my bunk, took the lid off both the black and white inkpad and took my name stamp out of its case. He dipped it into the white ink and stamped every bit of black kit right in the middle as it lay on the bunk and then repeated the same treatment to the white kit using the black ink.

"Re-scrub on Saturday morning." said FCCY Bracey.

Of course, everyone thought this was hilarious and for the next couple of years, until I grew out of my uniforms, I would have my name on display in unconventional locations on my kit. The ironic upside of this event was that my kit could never actually be stolen!

To my sixteen-year-old eyes, HMS Mercury was like a borstal, but much more fun. We all wore the same clothes, marched to and from classes and ate together in a large dining room. Most of the trainees were around my age and in order to ensure that we developed into strong young men, there was a great focus on sport. Our fitness, stamina and courage were tested regularly as most physical activities were monitored and recorded by either a watch or a counter. Runs had to be completed within a certain time and press-ups, push-ups and sit-ups had to reach a certain number.

Courage was assessed in the boxing ring. One day we were lined up in the gymnasium and told to pair off with someone around the same size. None of us had any boxing experience, so at least we were all in the same boat. We all knew what was coming and hushed deals were made.

"Okay, let's both take it easy and no hard punches."

These agreements generally lasted around 30 seconds until one or other of the combatants landed a solid blow and then it turned into a battle between two windmills. I don't recall who I was paired with, but I do remember deciding that I wasn't waiting to get hit. Due to my Northern Irish roots and accent, I'd been involved in a few fights, so I was fully aware that getting punched was painful and wasn't something I particularly liked. The bell went for the first round and within twenty seconds my opponent was on the canvas still trying to work out how he got there. My performance was convincing enough for me to be selected for the HMS Mercury boxing 'championships' later in the year.

The training also provided some interesting academic challenges. Repetitive skills such as morse code and typing were taught in specially designed labs and were hugely important, given that if you wanted to control which Communications sub-specialisation you entered, a certain standard had to be reached. General fleet training was also included, but as we were stuck up a windy hill in Hampshire, we hardly got our feet wet.

Chapter 27 – Bunting Tosser

Back then, there were four communications disciplines, all of which carried out the same initial training for the first nine weeks. After that you could choose which specialisation you preferred provided that your skills were up to it. For those who were good at morse code, RO(General) or RO(Submarine) was the way to go. If your morse skills were only average, then RO(Tactical) was the best option and for those whose dubious skills would make Samuel Morse himself turn in his grave then it was the RO(Warfare) route for you.

The training and continuous testing and exams also brought me stumbling into another startling realisation. I wasn't stupid! At that time in England, all jokes about 'thick' people were aimed at the Irish. "Paddy walks into a bar....", etc. Now I wasn't to know that this was a common link to other European countries – the Belgians vs the Dutch, the Portuguese vs the Spanish or the French vs the English. In any case, with the constant reference to thick Irishmen and the fact that I had no GCEs or any academic qualifications at all, I didn't have any great confidence in my level of intelligence. Then I started to come top of the class in the majority of our tests and exams. I also discovered that I could remember pretty much everything that was said in the classroom so didn't have to study in the evenings before exams. This was actually a Godsend, as I got to use those extra hours keeping my kit up to scratch and I eventually got to the point where I was passing my kit musters the first time around. I did sufficiently well in my academic and practical exams to select my sub-specialisation. I chose to become a Radio Operator (Tactical), whose main job at sea was as the communications operator on the bridge, which I believed to be the hub of the ship's operations. It also meant more time on the upper deck, rather than being stuck down between decks all the time. The RO(T) or Bunting Tosser, as he was affectionately known, because of his use of semaphore flags, was also required to master the use of flashing lights to send morse code messages from ship to ship. As the summer of 1975 drifted into autumn, we Buntings stood many an hour in the rain at HMS Mercury, trying to read the signal light from the corner of a building some distance away. We suddenly realised that being outside a lot more was not all that special!

Practicing my flashing light skills

If You Can't Take a Joke…

Chapter 28 – HMS Juno – Oh, Dear!

There was however, a bonus for doing well up to this point in my training. There was a gap of about two weeks between the end of initial communications training and the start of the final 13-week phase of Tactical training. Those trainees who did particularly well during initial training were offered the chance to take a few days training at sea on board an operational warship. I was allocated a ten-day trip in HMS Juno, a Leander class frigate. The Leanders were the backbone of the Royal Navy for two decades, with 26 ships built between 1959 and 1973, with the last one, HMS ARIADNE commissioned in February of that year. So the idea was for me to gain as much experience during that short trip as possible and I certainly did that, but possibly not the type of experiences that the Royal Navy had anticipated for the 16-year-old Junior Radio Operator Second Class (Tactical) or JRO2(T) Skull.

The trip started as well as can be expected, with my arriving on board at the right time, wearing the correct uniform and with the necessary kit. Of course, I was entering a whole new world, which appeared to assault all the senses. The ship itself was like a maze, with narrow, dark passageways, hatches and ladders to different compartments and over 260 crew all needing to be somewhere else. Everything I touched vibrated or shuddered and felt strangely warm. Pipes, signs, lockers and equipment covered every bulkhead (wall) and not a single item was without a label or marking. A typical hatch or door would have Damage Control Markings, which tell you exactly

If You Can't Take a Joke...

where on the ship it was situated and under which conditions it could be left open or had to be locked and secured with clips – the markings would often tell you exactly how many clips were to be used. There wasn't an area of the ship that didn't smell – not necessarily unpleasant, but heavy odours lingered throughout the ship and it seemed that the diesel fumes left a greasy coating on the tongue. Engines, generators, pumps and air-conditioning ensured that noise was your constant companion, punctuated by the slamming of hatches and the screeching, drumming and banging of various tools being used by the maintenance teams.

No sooner was I shown to the Communicators messdeck and allocated a bunk and locker, than we were called to Harbour Stations and got underway. This whole process was new to me and conducted in an entirely new sea-going language,

"Hands to Harbour Stations, Close all upper deck screen doors and hatches, hands out of rig of the day clear off the upper deck. Special sea-duty men close up, assume NBCD State 3 Condition Yankee!"

Luckily I was taken under the wing of one of the experienced ROs, who said,

"Just follow me, do what I do, don't say anything and don't touch anything!"

As with all things in the Royal Navy, every process had a detailed procedure and everything had to be done the same way every time. Those crew who weren't directly involved with actual handling ropes or carrying out specific sailing duties were lined up around the upper deck. As a signalman, I was stationed on the flag deck and had a great view of leaving Portsmouth Harbour – the first of many, many times. The front deck of the ship is called the forecastle, abbreviated to fo'c'sle and pronounced folk-sel and was a hive of activity. Seaman branch ratings readying lines to be either thrown off ashore or hauled inboard, getting the anchor ready to let go in the event of any emergency and a single tactical RO at the pointy end ready to haul down the Union Jack once the last line is ashore and the ship is 'at sea'. There has been some debate in modern times about the use of the term 'Union Jack' as opposed to 'Union Flag'. Throughout my time in the Royal Navy, it was considered that the flag should only be referred to as the Union Jack when flown on the Jack-staff at the fo'c'sle of warships. More recently in 2013 the Flag Institute, a charitable organisation concerned with vexillological issues that clearly mean a lot to some retired people with too much time on their hands and a penchant for words that mean little to normal people, declared that the terms Union Flag and Union Jack are simply interchangeable. Not on my watch.

As a Junior who had yet to complete his training, I was double-banked with an experienced operator. During this trip, which was purely a 'flying the flag' visit, we were not in company with other ships, so the bridge watches were very quiet, but it was an excellent opportunity for me to get a feel for life at sea. Sadly, I became more familiar with the feel of the cold steel of the bridge toilet, as sea-sickness struck and I spent much time 'talking to God on the big silver telephone'! Nevertheless, I managed to keep my watches and, the true

If You Can't Take a Joke…

test, satisfied the ship's communicators that I would be more than satisfactory as an addition to the fleet.

Two days later, the ship closed up at Harbour Stations and, with the assistance of Dutch tugs, we safely berthed alongside in Amsterdam – my first time out of the United Kingdom.

Amsterdam, of course, has always relished its reputation as the Hedonistic capital of Europe. Its lack of restraint both legally and morally in the partaking of Bacchanalian activities was legendary in the 1970s. By the way, I am not a scholar of Roman mythology and the only reason I feel qualified to use the word Bacchanalian is that my first ship's company role was in HMS Bacchante and we all had to know the history of our ships' names. Anyway back to Amsterdam. Prior to berthing alongside, the ship's Chaplain spoke to all the Junior Ratings in the ship, with the standard 'What you need to know before proceeding ashore' spiel. This warned us about which areas were considered seedy, immoral, dangerous and/or a combination of the three. In effect, this acted as a very early Lonely Planet guide informing us of exactly where we should be heading the moment we set foot on terra firma.

Still being under the age of 18, my leave was still restricted to midnight, so planning the run ashore was crucial. I had paired up with Thommo Thompson, a veteran of six years who knew all the angles.

"Don't worry about being back by midnight, Paddy. My oppo is the quartermaster during the middle watch and he'll let us slide on down to the mess."

If You Can't Take a Joke...

This meant that one of his close mates was manning the gangway between midnight and four in the morning and would turn a blind eye if I came back late. So with my best run ashore outfit donned, a sneaky tin or two of beer before heading off the ship and, in accordance with the Chaplains 'advice', a short taxi ride to De Wallen, the triple-P threat – pot, pints and prostitutes awaited! As a fresh faced 17-year old, all this coming at once left me with mixed feelings of angst and excitement. I'd never done drugs, was a bit of a lightweight drinker and, given my only previous sexual encounter was with Jean in Harwich, I was hardly a lothario when it came to the ladies. Well, I must confess that as the evening progressed, I became more relaxed and by the end of the night my triple-P achievements had reached the Meatloaf grade of 'Two out of Three Ain't Bad!'

I took to pot like a rock star and combined with copious amounts of alcohol, everything I said was simply hilarious and my dance moves would have put Nureyev to shame! Regarding the ladies, I won't go into too much detail, however I am reminded of the old navy joke:

Sailor to prostitute, "How am I doing?"

Prostitute replies, "You're in the Navy, aren't you?"

Sailor proudly, "Indeed I am!"

Prostitute, "Well, you're doing about three knots..."

Sailor, "Huh?"

Prostitute, "You're not in, you're not hard and you're not getting your money back!"

Clearly, I had some work to do in the art of love! Despite this, a great night was had by all and we started to make our way back to

If You Can't Take a Joke…

HMS Juno. I knew we were late, but felt confident because of Thommo's mate on the gangway. Being the most junior, smallest and more than likely the most drunk, I staggered up the gangway into the welcoming arms of the quartermaster. Sadly, it was now 4.30am and Thommo's mate had gone off watch 30 minutes previously and was by now warm and snug in his bunk. No special arrangement had been made with the new quartermaster,

"JRO Skull, I believe? One of HMS Mercury's finest, I understand. We've been waiting for you for four and a half hours. Nice of you to join us. Now off you go to bed and, oh yes, please report to the Joss at 08.00am!"

Chapter 29 – The Discipline Naval Act

The Naval Discipline Act 1957 (NDA) coupled with the Queen's Regulations for the Royal Navy (QRRN) cover every aspect of a sailor's existence ranging from the amount of alcohol that can be consumed daily by the various ratings and ranks to what materials must be used in the construction of coffins for burials at sea. However, one of the most common infractions of the NDA and QRRNs is the offence of absenting oneself from your place of duty or being 'adrift'. This isn't like the more serious offence of desertion, but simply being late. This offence is considered 'aggravated' if the ship is under sailing orders, i.e. within 24 hours of sailing. Clearly the implications of missing one's ship are severe. The degree of seriousness depends on the steps to be taken to get you back onboard. So if the ship's crew can see you waving frantically from the jetty as it sets off, a boat may be lowered to come and pick you up. Too late for that? If you can contact the ship by radio, they could send the ship's helicopter back to fetch you, but this is a bit more costly, both in operational terms and the penalty you will receive when charged. Worst case scenario (and this happened to one of my shipmates later in my career), after a great night out followed by a great night in, it appears he had fallen in love with a local girl in Sydney. He decided not to rejoin his ship as the thought of leaving his new Sheila was too much for him to bear. However, 24 hours later he realised he had just fallen in lust, rather than love, and better get back onboard before he is considered a deserter instead of just being adrift. Unfortunately, the ship had already sailed and was on her way to South Africa! He then had to go to the nearest British Embassy, explain the situation and have them issue a travel warrant all the way to Cape Town, so that he could rejoin the ship. Oh dear!

Although my transgression was only four and a half hours and I didn't actually miss the ship sailing, it was my first time 'in the shit' and I wasn't looking forward to my summary trial.

So, what exactly is a Royal Navy summary trial? Most people will have heard of a Court Martial and even seen examples in the movies....."YOU CAN'T HANDLE THE TRUTH!" (Jack Nicholson – A Few Good Men), but these are generally trials for more serious offences. It was impractical to send sailors ashore for trials at Magistrates' Courts and, in any case, many misdemeanours considered punishable in the Royal Navy were not even offences in civilian life. For example, being five minutes late for work at Boots the Chemist would not see you formally charged. In the 1970s, transgressions worthy of a trial in the Royal Navy included:

- Insubordination (basically disagreeing with any opinion, suggestion or order of any superior rate or rank)
- Being drunk (not necessarily disorderly)
- Malingering (being judged to be not working hard enough)
- Not shaving or having hair below the line of the collar

In order to be suitably punished for these offences, it was necessary to have a judicial system in which an offence could be investigated, charged and punished onboard the ship – summary trial.

So, when my first ever foreign run ashore ended with the Quartermaster ordering me to, "...please report to the Joss at

If You Can't Take a Joke…

8.00am", the legal system in HMS JUNO swung into action. Given the fact that I was not part of the permanent Ship's Company, but more a guest, my offence was considered particularly onerous. Dragging myself out of my pit at 7.45am for my appointment, I was already terrified that I was likely to be charged with 'absent without leave' and I was hungover and I only had two and a half hours sleep and I was feeling very sorry for myself and I hated Thommo and his fucking mate, who was supposed to be on the gangway! I should explain at this point that the Joss or Jossman is a member of the Service Police and holds the rank of Master-at-Arms, addressed as 'Master', and is responsible for discipline and security onboard the ship. He is also the arbiter of what charges should be laid against offenders who breach the Queen's Regulations for the Royal Navy. Our meeting didn't go well.

I waited nervously outside his office, trying desperately not to throw up from the effects of both my hangover and my predicament. Outside the Jossman's office was a full-length mirror, so that you could check that your appearance was properly 'squared-away' before you visit the ship's policeman. What I was supposed to see in the mirror was a fine example of a British seafarer, broad of chest and with a twinkle in his eye. The reality was a boy, barely 17 years-old, his uniform hanging off his skinny frame like kid playing dress-up. My eyes were bloodshot and my head felt like I was wearing an internal balaclava made of steel wool. Finally, a voice rang out from the office,

"JRO SKULL! GET IN HERE YOU WORTHLESS PIECE OF SHIT!"

I marched into his office and stood smartly to attention in front of his desk. It became quickly evident that the Joss had no volume control,

"WHERE'S YOUR FUCKING BERET?"

"Oh sorry, Master, I didn't think I'd need it."

"WELL, CLEARLY 'NOT THINKING' IS BECOMING A BIT OF A FUCKING HABIT, ISN'T IT? CHARGE ONE – NOT WEARING PROPER UNIFORM."

"But, Master, I don't think that's really fair…"

"AND THERE YOU GO NOT THINKING AGAIN! CHARGE TWO – INSUBORDINATION. NOW, WHAT TIME DID TO GRACE US WITH YOUR PRESENCE LAST NIGHT…OR SHOULD I SAY THIS MORNING?"

"I don't really know, but I'm sure you already have that information or I wouldn't be here."

I have no idea what possessed me to say that. The Joss stood up and leaned across his desk. With his face inches from mine,

"ARE YOU TAKING THE PISS? YOU THINK THIS IS FUCKING FUNNY?"

"No, sorry."

His face was still so close to mine that I could smell his breakfast, but his expression changed from anger to something more quizzical, as he examined my down-covered visage,

"DID YOU SHAVE THIS MORNING?"

"Eh, no. I normally only have to shave every two or three days."

"GOD FUCKING SAVE US. CHARGE THREE – GROWING A BEARD WITHOUT PERMISSION!"

Even though I knew that I couldn't grow a beard to save my life, I kept quiet. I suspected this wasn't quite over.

"NOW, WHAT THE FUCK HAPPENED LAST NIGHT?"

"Well, Master, I went ashore with the lads and we had a few drinks. I guess I lost track of time."

"SO, YOU'RE FUCKING 17 YEARS-OLD. CHARGE FOUR – CONSUMPTION OF ALCOHOL WHILST UNDERAGE AND CHARGE FIVE – ABSENTING YOURSELF WITHOUT LEAVE. THE QUEEN'S REGULATIONS DON'T ALLOW ME TO CHARGE YOU WITH BEING A FUCKING SAD REFLECTION ON THE COUNTRY, MY NAVY, THIS SHIP OR YOUR FUCKING FAMILY, SO GET THE FUCK OUT OF MY OFFICE AND REPORT FOR CAPTAIN'S TABLE AT 1100 HOURS. ABOUT TURN, QUICK MARCH!"

With my cheeks burning with embarrassment and humiliation and my eyes stinging with salty tears, I quickly about turned and quick marched back to the messdeck trying my best not to cry.

The next stage of my 'trial' was appearing at the Captain's table. This stage is also known as 'Wheel the Guilty Bastard In'. The Captain delivered his conclusions of my behaviour, which were entirely in accord with the Master-at-Arms, but more refined in his delivery. Found guilty of all charges, I was sentenced to:

- One week's forfeiture of pay
- Stoppage of shore leave for one week

- Seven days of Number 9 Punishment (two hours extra work per day and reporting to the Master-at-Arms three times per day, so that he could assess my remorse)

The effect of these punishments were that for the last week of my time aboard HMS JUNO, I was confined to the ship and worked like a dog. What a great reward for the sterling results of my initial training exams! At least, I thought, it has now been dealt with and I'll learn from the experience, take the punishment, then put the whole sorry episode behind me. Little did I know!

Chapter 30 – Double Jeopardy

The completion of my punishment regime on HMS JUNO coincided with my return to HMS MERCURY to continue my communications training. My reputation had preceded me, as they say. As I rejoined the communications school, the first instruction I was given was to report to the establishment Master-at-Arms. Once again I found myself standing outside the Joss's office and heard the now familiar refrain,

"JRO SKULL, GET IN HERE. QUICK MARCH!"

It became quickly apparent that reports of my performance in Amsterdam had carried swiftly through the communications channels and, even though I had completed my penance aboard HMS JUNO, more was to come. Basically, I went through exactly the same procedure, but with only one charge being forthcoming. It was declared that during my time on that ship, I was effectively an ambassador for HMS MERCURY and had brought shame and disgrace upon the establishment and was charged with bringing its good name into disrepute. Thankfully, the stoppage of pay, curtailment of leave and extra work onboard HMS JUNO was taken into consideration and the Captain 'awarded' me only another seven days stoppage of leave. This was not a major impediment given that I was in the middle of training and HMS MERCURY was in the middle of nowhere, so I wouldn't be going anywhere in any case.

It had been a traumatic couple of weeks. I was feeling somewhat out of place. I did not seem to be fitting in as well as the rest of the

If You Can't Take a Joke…

trainees and although I was doing very well in the training, with excellent exam results, I began to feel that this whole Navy malarkey might have been an error. I was still within my first six months of service, so had the option of giving two weeks' notice to leave. Once the six months mark was passed, I would have to give 18 months' notice to leave. At 17 years-old, 18 months sounded like a lifetime. After my poor showing on HMS JUNO, I was convinced that I lacked the discipline and commitment for a career in the Royal Navy and filled in my application to leave and left it in the in-box of my Divisional Officer, Fleet Chief Communications Yeoman (FCCY) Chris Bracey.

The following morning, FCCY Bracey sent a message that I should see him in his office. His reputation was that of a strict, no-nonsense, old-school disciplinarian and he was universally loathed and feared in equal measures. I was sure that I was going to receive a severe bollocking calling into question my manhood, intelligence and judgement, but when I arrived in his office on a Friday afternoon, he was sitting quietly in his chair, his tie removed and the top button of his shirt undone,

"Have a seat, young Skull."

I took the seat across from him, sitting bolt upright. He smiled,

"Okay, it's Friday afternoon and instruction has finished for the week, so for fuck sake relax."

I didn't. He held up my application and continued,

"Look, it's Friday, so I won't be doing anything with this until Monday morning, so I'd like you to take the weekend to think long and hard about whether or not you really want to proceed with submitting your notice application. I've had a look at your record and I think you might be making a big mistake. Your exam results are excellent and, apart from that nonsense in Amsterdam, you've pretty much kept your nose clean. If you stay and knuckle down, you could have a bright career ahead of you. Think about that and also think about the life you'll be going back to if you decide to leave. If on Monday morning you feel the same way, I'll submit your application and backdate it to today, so you won't even have to do more time. Okay?"

I knew deep down that I would not change my mind, but wasn't brave enough to argue with FCCY Bracey.

"Okay, Sir, thank you, Sir."

I spent most of the weekend preparing for the next week's course work, as even though I was leaving, I would still have to work my two weeks' notice by continuing training. By Sunday afternoon, my resolve was still intact and I had started thinking about what I would do next. At around four o'clock, Mr. Bracy knocked on our mess door and stuck his head round. Everyone jumped off their chairs or beds and stood to attention.

"Stand at ease, everyone. Young Skull, could you join me outside, please?"

I followed him out of the building to find him standing beside my mother and Alan, who had just driven up from Bournemouth. Mum stepped forward,

"Hello, son. How are you?"

If You Can't Take a Joke...

I was totally taken aback and struggled to speak,

"Yeah, good, I suppose. What are you doing here, Mum?"

Mr. Bracey interrupted,

"I telephoned your mother and told her about you wanting to leave. Because you are a Junior, I have a responsibility to ensure that the Navy releases you into a safe, secure and welcoming environment. Having met your parents, I now have no concerns on that count. However, I did feel that it is right and proper that you speak with them about this decision before you and I meet formally tomorrow morning. After all, it is going to affect them, too. Now, I will leave you alone to have a chat. Eight o'clock tomorrow, JRO Skull."

With that, he executed a perfect 180-degree about turn and marched off leaving us alone.

As the three of us strolled along, we chatted about what had happened to me over the past few months – the failed kit musters, the good exam results, my growing confidence and even the fiasco in Amsterdam. Mum and Alan didn't really voice any opinion as to whether or not I should leave, but listened intently as I talked about my reasons for leaving. It was funny, but when I explained my feelings aloud, the reasons appeared to become more and more trivial. I also realized that I really didn't miss home that much. Alan reminded me of the high unemployment rate and Mum mentioned that Fred was enjoying having his own room. Clearly, they did not miss me that much either! After a while, conversation was overtaken by uncomfortable silences and we suddenly found ourselves standing in the car park beside their car. Farewells were exchanged and I watched them unemotionally as they drove away.

As ordered, at 8.00am on Monday morning, I was standing to attention outside FCCY Bracey's office. His voice rang out,

"JRO SKULL, in you come!"

I marched in and stood to attention in front of his desk. He held my application to leave the Royal Navy in his outstretched hand and asked,

"Right, what am I to do with this?"

I reached across and took it from him. I looked at it for a moment and tore it in two, then four pieces. He held up his wastepaper bin,

"Good decision, young Skull. NOW GET THE FUCK OUT OF MY OFFICE AND BACK TO FUCKING WORK!"

Then, he winked!

Chapter 31 – Life in a Blue Suit

The next few weeks flew by, as did the six-month point and the two-week notice 'escape clause'. Now I was fully committed to the Royal Navy, or at the very least for the next 18 months. As recommended by Mr. Bracey, I did in fact knuckle down and continued to perform well during the later stages of training. My confidence grew and the shy loner from Belfast slowly became Paddy Skull, as John Skull receded into the past.

I was not an angel, by any means, but my scrapes, scraps and rule infringements went largely undetected or were dealt with informally by a swift kick-up-the-arse from various instructors.

I started to change physically as well. In the last three months of my training at HMS Mercury, I had an enormous and rapid growth spurt. When I joined HMS GANGES, my medical records noted an 8-stones underweight lad, who stood 5-feet 7-inches tall – what you might call a runt. After the endless physical training, marching, sports and healthy diet, within nine months I was 5-feet 11-inches tall and respectable 10-stones. Look out world!

Throughout our training, we would occasionally lose recruits. Some found the disciplinarian regime too tough, some did not meet the educational or physical fitness requirement and yet others were medically discharged. For those of us that remained, our thoughts turned to our first posting to an operational ship of the Royal Navy. In early-December 1975, we huddled around the noticeboard to see what lay ahead. Posting, or drafting in Naval parlance, took into account a number of issues, like where the rating lived, how well he performed during training and, of course, operational requirements. Scottish recruits, for example, would likely find themselves on ships based in Rosyth or Faslane, whereas English recruits would be based in the English dockyards at Chatham, Portsmouth or Plymouth. My personal preference, which was not one of the issues taken into consideration, was for a proper warship. I dreaded the thought of being sent to a Fisheries Protection Patrol ship or even a small minesweeper, which plied their trade in waters around the United Kingdom. I wanted guns, missiles and a thrusting, steel harbinger of death, thrashing the oceans to a white froth and flying the White Ensign to all corners of the globe. Hoorah!

One by one, we peeled away from the noticeboard as we learned of our nautical fate, with diverse reactions:

"Faslane! Fuck me, I joined to get away from Scotland!"

"Fishery Protection? What are we protecting the fucking fish from?"

"Aircraft carrier..woo hoo!!!"

Next to my name on the roster was, 'HMS BACCHANTE – 5th January 1976'. I was delighted – Woo Hoo! BACCHANTE was a Leander Class Frigate, the same class as HMS JUNO of Amsterdam-fame, so I had some idea of what to expect. This meant that all I had to do was complete the last two weeks of training, survive Christmas leave at home and off I would go into the wild blue yonder. The news got even better. After finding out which ship we were drafted to, we headed to the Admin Block to check the Forward Operations Planner

If You Can't Take a Joke...

(FOP) to check the ships' programmes for the following year. HMS BACCHANTE's programme looked like the holiday of a lifetime. Sailing from Chatham on 6th January, followed by port visits including Gibraltar, Sardinia, Naples, Malta and Alexandria, to name just a few. I could not believe my luck. Many were less fortunate, with some joining ships due for long refits in the various dockyards in the UK, which for a Junior Rating meant months of chipping paint, scrubbing, sanding, varnishing and repainting. For others, on Fishery Protection vessels, they would enjoy endless patrols in the North Sea and North Atlantic in the coldest stormiest months of the year on small ships. Haha, but for me it was to be the blue skies, calm seas and exotic ports of the Mediterranean Sea. I recalled the recruitment poster at the traffic lights of almost a year ago and I was about to become that sailor! The last two weeks of training dragged on interminably, as I was impatient to leave the training environment. I was becoming increasingly confident in my abilities, having done very well in all aspects of the final exams. I still couldn't spit and polish my shoes to the required standard, nor was I remotely as squared away as the shiny sailor, who met me at Ipswich Rail Station ten months previously, but I was ready for the fleet and raring to go. Constant rehearsals for our passing out parade on a cold and rainy hill in Hampshire was doing little to prepare me for the sun and heat of the Mediterranean, but the formalities of passing out and leave routines were soon complete and before I knew it, I was heading back to Ferndown and my family for Christmas leave. My return to the family fold didn't cause any particular upheaval, as I recall, but neither was it a major celebration.

Fred was a little disgruntled that he had to share his, not our, bedroom. The only point of friction was quickly resolved, when Fred became angry and threatened to give me a hiding. I had had ten months of tough and prolonged physical training since we last shared a room and I remember standing up and facing him. I was now taller and stockier than him,

"Not today, Fred."

I had become used to days filled with activity in classrooms, on the parade ground and in the gym, but at home, the days were long, empty and boring and I could not wait to join my ship on the 5th of January. As luck would have it, I didn't have to wait that long. On the morning of 28th December, we were all having breakfast. The phone rang and Alan answered it. He returned to the table, untangling the long telephone cord and passing me the handset,

"It's for you, John, he asked for JRO Skull."

I took the phone,

"Eh, hello, this is JRO Skull", I said, secretly hoping that I was impressing my family by using my rank and receiving a call from Her Majesty's Royal Navy.

"Happy Christmas, JRO Skull, this is the Master-at-Arms from HMS BACCHANTE."

Just for a moment, I thought that my adventures in Amsterdam and subsequent punishments at Mercury were about to have a sequel, but mercifully the Master-at-Arms continued in a surprisingly pleasant voice,

If You Can't Take a Joke...

"I hope you haven't got too much planned for New Year's Eve, Skull. The ship's programme has changed and you are needed onboard tomorrow by noon. Is that going to be a problem?"

Even if I had had a party planned with the First Sea Lord, there is only ever one answer to that question,

"Of course not, Master. Can I ask if we're sailing earlier to Gibraltar?"

Some things never change, do they?

"NO YOU CAN'T FUCKING ASK. DO YOU THINK I'M GOING TO DISCLOSE CLASSIFIED MOVEMENTS OF ONE OF HER MAJESTY'S SHIPS ON AN INSECURE TELEPHONE LINE? MERRY CHRISTMAS AND DON'T BE FUCKING LATE!"

Shit, shit, shit……

"Same to you Master, I mean the Merry Christmas bit……"

He had already hung up. Looking back, I am so glad that speakerphones had not been invented by then.

That phonecall saved me another uncomfortable week at home. My naval kit was already packed up in my kitbag, so all I needed was a small bag for my T-shirts and shorts. My previous experiences had made me paranoid about being adrift, so I decided to head off early that afternoon. Even though only the Sunday services were running, I would not risk any mishap the next day. Warm, if not loving, farewells were made in the driveway and then Alan drove me to Bournemouth Station. He helped me retrieve my bags from the boot and we stood awkwardly at the kerbside. He wished me luck and we shook hands.

If You Can't Take a Joke...

As I stood on the platform waiting for the train, my Royal Navy kitbag on the ground at my feet, my usual feelings of apprehension and anxiety were inexplicably absent. In their place were feelings of confidence, achievement and pride. I was no longer a child, or an apprentice or a trainee. I was Junior Radio Operator (Tactical) 2nd Class John Richard Skull, D150511R, crew of HMS BACCHANTE in Her Majesty's Royal Navy. Hoorah!

HMS BACCHANTE – My first ship

Chapter 32 – If You Can't Take a Joke, You Shouldn't Have Joined!

After an uneventful trip lugging my increasingly heavy kitbag across the city, from Waterloo to Victoria station on the London Underground, I boarded the train for Chatham. In 1975, Chatham Naval Dockyard, with its accompanying shore establishment HMS Pembroke were major Royal Naval facilities and the Victoria to Chatham line always had a decent smattering of naval personnel as passengers. Even though most travelled in civilian attire, the large mustard-coloured kitbag was a dead giveaway. In order to protect the stiff wire frame of his cap, a sailor would secure it onto the outside of his kitbag. The cap is adorned with a black silk ribbon around its circumference and this 'tally' is embroidered in gold with the ship's name. As I staggered along the swaying and rattling carriages looking for the smoking carriage, I spotted a sailor with an HMS BACCHANTE cap on his bag. His feet were up on the seat opposite and he drew casually on his cigarette. Of course, the old John Skull wouldn't have dreamed of approaching him, but things had changed. I approached him casually,

"Mind if I join you, mate?"

He saw my kitbag, stubbed out his cigarette and took his feet of the seat opposite,

"Fill yer boots, mate. Have a seat."

I hefted my kitbag into the overhead rack and slumped into the seat opposite and pointed to his cap,

If You Can't Take a Joke…

"You off HMS BACCHANTE, then?"

"Oh, no," he replied, "I nicked this off a drunken matelot last night!" He paused, for a moment, then,

"'Course I am, you numpty!"

He winked and stuck out his hand,

"Butch Butcher, best Golly on the good ship BACCHANTE!"

I laughed and shook his hand firmly,

"Paddy Skull, joining as Ship's Company in the morning. Earlier than I expected, though."

Butch took out his box of cigarettes, flipped open the top and offered me the box,

"Here you go, shippers. Yeah, we've all been called off leave early. Change of plan. Probably sail as soon as we have enough crew onboard – maybe even tomorrow night. First draft for you, I suppose?"

Butch was probably no more than two years older than I was, but he had a casual, cool maturity that belied his youth. Easy-going and friendly, too, so we whiled away the hour or so to Chatham chatting about our Christmas leave. As we approached Chatham Station, he said,

"Hey, Paddy, it's going to be a proper fucking zoo when we get to the ship, what with the early recall, but if you stick to me like shit to a blanket, I'll get you sorted. We're in the same messdeck, so don't get your knickers in a twist, okay?"

"Sure, Butch. Thanks."

If You Can't Take a Joke...

We had agreed to share a taxi down to the Dockyard, but as I headed towards the taxi-rank, Butch pulled me back,

"Fuck me, Paddy, you really are a sprog. Okay, Chatham lesson number one. Taxi drivers hate matelots. Firstly, if it is after 10pm, we're generally pissed as farts. Secondly, we are shit tippers and thirdly, if we are at the Station, it means we are going to the Dockyard. That's a one mile trip, low fare and no tip. If they spot a kitbag, off goes the 'For Hire' light. Taxi drivers fucking hate matelots, got it?"

I chuckled and nodded. Butch left me standing out of sight with both kitbags and approached the taxi rank. He opened the door and got into the front passenger seat, turned around and shouted,

"Okay, Paddy, out you come, son!"

I sped over as quickly as I could, dragging both kitbags. I hoisted them into the boot and jumped into the front seat, beside the driver,

"Dockyard, please mate, HMS BACCHANTE, number 3 Basin."

We flashed our ID cards to the Ministry of Defence Police stationed at the dockyard gates and the driver stopped at the bottom of HMS BACCHANTE's gangway. We jumped out, grabbed our kitbags from the boot and Butch paid the driver the exact amount of the fare.

"Fucking skates!" the driver muttered as he departed.

It was now early evening and activities onboard were winding down. Unable to carry out any sort of joining routine and with Butch greasing the skids, I soon found myself in the messdeck, which was to be my home for the next 18 months, or so.

If You Can't Take a Joke...

The HMS BACCHANTE Communications Department messdeck was in a different location to that on HMS JUNO. Two decks down from the main deck, it was accessed by a deck hatch and ladder. Imagine a tin of sardines, then squeeze out the oil or tomato juice and cram in a couple more sardines. The bunks were arranged in triple-racks around the mess square, effective the living room, with an offshoot for the senior members of the mess – the Leading Hands, known as Killicks. This is an old English word for stone or rock used to anchor boats and was adopted as slang for Leading Hands, because their rank badge consisted of an anchor. Leander-class frigates were designed in the 1950's and HMS BACCHANTE itself was about ten years old. The ceilings, or deckheads, were a monkey-puzzle of pipes, wiring conduits and air-conditioning vents, all painted white, but now stained to a nicotine yellow, like an old pub ceiling. The deck itself consisted of green, polished vinyl tiles. Harsh fluorescents provided the lighting, notice-boards with various memoranda added to the décor and a mixture of diesel oil, tobacco smoke and stale body-odour rounded off the warship ambience. The most senior of the Leading Hands was the Killick-of-the Mess, and he was responsible for the good order and disciple of the members of his mess. His name was Tim Cranham and, like me, he was a bunting-tosser, albeit far more senior. There were about 25 sailors in our mess, mostly communicators, but with a few interlopers, such as the ship's Writers and the Medical Assistant. I was allocated one of the bottom bunks with an adjacent locker. Unlike HMS JUNO, I was now permanent Ship's Company and was warmly welcomed. My messmates were

If You Can't Take a Joke…

starting to settle down for the evening. In one corner, a young sailor had his guitar and was knocking out a fair-to-middling rendition of Ralph McTell's 'Streets of London', with a few of his mates joining in the chorus, whilst others played cards and had a beer or two. Handshakes and words of welcome were offered and LRO Cranham told me I'd best get my kit unpacked into my locker and bags stowed away, as I wouldn't be needing them for the foreseeable future. The naval kit from my kitbag was quickly stowed away, exactly as it had been in Ganges and Mercury and as I started to unpack my civvies, one of my new messmates noticed that the bulk of my 'going ashore' rig consisted of shorts and T-shirts. He tapped me on the shoulder,

"Hey, Paddy, you look a bit light on the old civvies, mate."

I held up my favourite Led Zeppelin T-shirt,

"Well this is all I'll need in the sunny Mediterranean, shippers!"

Laughing hysterically, led me to the mess-square and banged on the table for attention,

"Hey, lads, young Paddy here, our latest arrival is all kitted out for the Med. Who's gonna tell him the good news?"

As one, the entire mess burst into raucous laughter and Butch pushed himself towards me, putting his arm around my shoulder,

"Oh, poor Paddy! Mate, the early recall for you and the rest of the crew is because of a programme change. We're going to war!"

I was astounded. War? I'm only 17 and I joined for the fun, travel and companionship, not fucking war! I blurted out,

"War? I didn't know we are at war. I didn't see anything in the papers!"

If You Can't Take a Joke...

More thigh-slapping laughter continued and then Butch enlightened me,

"Yep, we're sailing on Friday and we're not heading south to the Med, we're headed for the North Atlantic. We going to save the fish…welcome to the Cod War with Iceland!"

I was dumbstruck, but a sudden shout caught my attention,

"Here, Paddy, catch!"

I caught the can of beer that was thrown to me. Another voice,

"A toast, Paddy, old mate. If you can't take a joke, you shouldn't have joined!"

I couldn't help but laugh and raised my beer,

"If you can't take a joke, you shouldn't have joined."

As most of the lads had just returned from leave, they had plenty of catching up to do and on my first evening onboard, I sat quietly in the background getting to know my new shipmates. Tomorrow was the beginning of preparing the ship and her crew for a new operational role in the North Atlantic, during the coldest, roughest time of the year.

Chapter 33 – There's No 'I' in Team

The next few days was a hectic mix of manual labour, joining routines and operational preparation. A Royal Navy warship is everything to everyone. The needs of all onboard had to be accessible hundreds of miles from land, so the ship takes on the characteristics of a small town. In addition to all the navigation, weaponry, communications and propulsion systems required to allow a ship to fight effectively, in the event of conflict, the everyday needs of over 250 men also had to be provided. Electricity, heating, lighting, water, food, bedding, hygiene facilities and even sewerage were managed from within. Other more personal issues were address by the Chaplain, the Medical Assistant, the Chinese laundrymen and the NAAFI (Navy Army and Airforce Institute) Canteen Manager were as important as the Navigation Officer to ensure the effective running of HMS BACCHANTE. Although the most junior of the twenty or so ratings in the Communications (Comms) Department, I was part of the Comms team and was expected to pull my weight. On 2nd January 1976, we left Chatham Dockyard, transited the Medway River into the Thames Estuary and by early evening we were heading north towards Scotland in the very rough North Sea.

The reason we were heading in that direction was because of a dispute between Iceland and the United Kingdom, specifically over fishing rights. The north Atlantic waters had been rich fishing grounds for British fishermen since the 15th century, braving gales and monstrous seas. The advent of steam power in the latter half on the

19th century increased the number and frequency of British trawlers off Iceland and the ongoing political wrangles continue into the 20th century. Between the 1950s and 1970s, Iceland continued to declare increases in what they considered Icelandic Territorial Waters, starting at a modest four nautical miles in 1952. In 1958, this was further increased to 12 nautical miles and resulted in the First Cod War – a somewhat glorified title for what effectively became known as 'militarised interstate disputes' in United Nations jargon. Iceland won. Clearly feeling encouraged, they then increased their claim to Territorial Waters out to 50 nautical miles in 1972, but undaunted, the British once again disputed this claim and again the Royal Navy were sent up north. Iceland won. Having now won two Cod Wars, without a shot being fired in anger, the Icelanders went the whole hog in November 1975 and declared that their Territorial Waters now extended to 200 nautical miles. They clearly had no idea the JRO2(T) Paddy Skull was at that time undergoing Naval Training! Had they seen me hanging over the guardrail on that first night at sea, providing a free meal for the local British fish of the North Sea, they may have relaxed somewhat.

The duties of Comms Department ratings consisted of two elements – On Watch and Off Watch. On Watch entailed carrying out specialized communications functions, while Off Watch duties were any number of ongoing maintenance tasks, ranging from cleaning and painting, to assisting in the Junior Rates Dining Hall after mealtimes. As a Tactical communications rating, my On Watch station was on the bridge. Although the Operations Room, two decks below, was were all the radar, sonar, Electronic Warfare and weapons systems data were analysed and tactical decisions made, the bridge was where the navigation and ship-handling happened. I loved working on the bridge. The Watch consisted of the Officer of the Watch (OOW), the 2nd OOW (2OOW), the Quartermaster (QM), the Bosun's Mate (BM) and the Tactical Radio Operator(RO). I admired the slickness of the bridge team, with everyone knowing his role and the absolute trust they had in each other. The OOW was effectively the Captain's representative and when on Watch, had responsibility for the general running of the ship, including navigation, signals correspondence, adherence to the International Regulations for the Prevention of Collisions at Sea and keeping the Commanding Officer appraised of all relevant matters. The 2OOW was his right-hand man and was generally a junior officer either under training or gaining experience. He was in charge of the navigation chart and was required to maintain the Ship's Log. The Quartermaster (QM) was a Leading Hand, and manned the bridge telephone switchboard, handling enquiries from all departments in the ship. He also made the periodic announcements throughout the ship on the tannoy system. The Bosun's Mate (BM), whose most important role was to make tea for the bridge team, assisted him. As the Tactical Comms rating (RO), I manned the ship's radio systems, including standard Marine VHF and military systems, primarily encrypted HF. Depending on the operational status, I found myself speaking with other warships, commercial vessels, military aircraft and even oil-rigs. In addition to voice communications, I was also proficient in Morse Code (either by light or radio signal) and Flag

If You Can't Take a Joke…

Signaling. Oddly, there was no ship's wheel or engine controls on the bridge and the OOW had to use internal comms to talk to the helmsman, who was two decks below the bridge and had no windows. The OOW would provide not only the course to steer, but also the exact angle of wheel to be used. The two-way conversation would go something like this:

OOW:	Bridge to Wheelhouse
Helm:	Wheelhouse, Sir
OOW:	Starboard 10 (degrees of helm), altering 270
Helm:	Starboard 10, Sir, altering 270

Once the helmsman, who could not see where he was steering, saw that the compass was approaching the new course:

Helm:	Passing 250, Sir
OOW:	Roger, wheel amidships, steer 270
Helm:	Course 270

The vast majority of the crew spent most of their time below decks, particularly during rough weather, when the upper deck was put out of bounds in order to prevent sailors being tossed overboard. By being on the bridge, I was not only at the centre of activity, I could see the horizon and that is considered the best antidote to the dreaded scourge of sea-sickness. If you have never suffered from this particular condition, it is probably difficult to understand the impact it has on every single element of your day-to-day existence. It starts with a general feeling of lethargy, progresses to a sensation of impending death and finally results in kneeling in front of a toilet, heaving until your stomach is devoid of any matter whatsoever. First comes your

If You Can't Take a Joke…

last meal, then the naturally occurring digestive juices of your whole gastrointestinal system. You'd think that that would be the end of it, but no. Your body continues to spasm, so much so that you fully expect your lungs, kidneys and liver to join everything else in the toilet bowl. One day, we were carrying out training exercises that required us all to don our gas masks. These were heavy rubber masks with an airtight seal around the whole face, large lenses in front of the eyes and secured tightly to the head by rubber straps. In order to test the efficacy of these masks, the exercise staff had long sticks with a burning candle at the end that, instead of smoke, released CS gas fumes. These were waved around the mask to see if they leaked. One poor sod was suffering heavily from sea-sickness, when one of the staff came behind him and started waving the stick. Sadly, the victim's mask was faulty and he suddenly started reacting to the gas. I could visibly see his whole body starting to heave, as the gas triggered another bout of seasick heaving. He was between a rock and a hard place. If he removed his mask, he would be exposed to the CS gas and if he left it on, he was likely to vomit in his mask. He chose the latter option and I started to feel queasy myself when I saw the prolonged heave of his stomach contents starting to fill his mask. The second heave saw his lunch reach the lenses of his mask and I watched as the vomit level rose like a pint pot filling with frothy beer. The final and most explosive heave brought revenge on the instigator of his predicament. The mask had reached capacity and now jets of fresh spew jetted out of the straps of the mask and all over the staff member, who was still standing behind him. Sweet, sweet justice, I thought as I joined my shipmate at the guardrail and once again provided the fish with a free meal.

Chapter 34 – War is Hell, but Colder!

After a couple of days in Rosyth dockyard taking on final stores, including Artic clothing, we finally set off up the east coast of Scotland, altered course westwards between the Orkney and Shetland Island towards the Faroes and the North Atlantic. The sea state increased and the temperatures plummeted. It seemed like we were sailing in a perpetual gale and the temperatures were well below freezing. We were warned to stay off the upper deck, as falling overboard in these conditions would inevitably result in death. The first problem was that the water temperature was so cold that the human body would only manage about five minutes before succumbing. The major concern for me, however, was the mountainous seas, the ship would be unlikely to turn across the waves to come back to rescue you. After the initial week of rough weather, I had conquered my seasickness and enjoyed the excitement of the storms. Watching waves, with frothing whitecaps higher than the bridge and feeling the sensation of two and a half thousand tons of warship climb up the front of a wave and then slam violently into the trough behind was exhilarating. My biggest concern was capsizing. Frigates are very long and thin and they roll easily with the sea. Sleeping became difficult, as the ship rolled up to 50 degrees back and forth, making my bunk feel more like a washing machine than a bed.

If You Can't Take a Joke...

Relentless operations exercises, bridge watchkeeping duties and constant cleaning, scraping, polishing and painting resulted in 12-hour working days, seven days a week. As with many workers in high-stress occupations, like police, nurses and firefighters, one of the methods we employed to maintain our sanity was by playing pranks and with humour – often quite dark. Although a formidable band of brothers, not everyone was universally liked. One particular member of our mess was a rather glum and cantankerous sailor nicknamed Rattler, because of his penchant for purposely irritating his messmates – rattling their cages. To the delight of everyone else, he suffered terribly from hemorrhoids, to the point where he even had a rubber 'doughnut' to sit on to ease the pain. He would constantly berate the ship's Medical Assistant (MA) for not providing him effective medication for his condition, until one day the medic had had enough. He announced to Rattler,

"I've just been sent some new medication, somewhat experimental, for hemorrhoids. It's supposed to be very good, so would you like to give it a go?"

Rattler's piles were being particularly troublesome that day, so he leapt at the chance.

"Okay," said the MA, "Because it is an experimental ointment, I'll have to apply it myself, as I have to document exact dosage and circumstances when it is used. Meet me in the sickbay in half-an-hour."

The MA headed off to the Sick Bay, but he was not alone. One of the regular victims of Rattler's bullying behaviour, Shady Lane, accompanied him. The Sick Bay was not particularly well equipped, but it had a hospital bed, a toilet and a curtained shower cubicle, which was located directly adjacent to the sink. Shady hid in the shower and both he and the medic awaited the arrival of Rattler. At this juncture, I should say that the medic did actually have a new ointment for the treatment of piles. It will soon become apparent why I make this point. Rattler arrived soon after and was instructed by the medic to drop his trousers and lean over the sink with both hands, while he applied the cream. Rattler leaned on the sink and bent over. The MA put one hand on his shoulder and said,

"Ok, Rattler, it might sting a little, so I'll count you down…three, two…one…"

At this exact moment, Shady reached out of the shower and placed a hand on Rattler's other shoulder, as the medic sank two ointment-covered fingers into Rattler's rectum. One can only imagine his confusion, when he suddenly had a hand on each shoulder and something else disappearing up his arse! He, predictably, jumped entirely to the wrong conclusion!

It appeared to me that in addition to my recent physical growth spurt, I was also enjoying somewhat of a personality and confidence spurt. Our working hours were long and physically exhausting. Just fighting against the constant pitching and rolling of the ship resulting in bashing continually into bulkheads and hatches. Climbing ladders was particularly hazardous, as when the ship was pitching upwards it felt like I weighed 15 tons and then on the downward slam into the troughs of waves, I had to fight to stay on the ladder, as it was the same effect as weightlessness one feels as a roller-coaster plummets down the rails. The biggest challenge, by far, was simply staying awake during the wee small hours of the morning in the Radio Operators position on the bridge. Tiredness and the rocking motion quickly brought on drowsiness and I would suddenly jerk awake, having dozed off. This was not an option, as falling asleep on watch was considered a particularly heinous offence. By day, we dashed around the North Atlantic attempting to intercept Icelandic gunboats, whose tactics during the Cod War was to cut the nets of British trawlers, which would then have to return to the UK for repairs. This involved some extremely close encounters in very rough seas and a number of Royal Navy frigates were holed during these manoeuvres. Of course, this was not a war in the traditional sense, where we could simply launch a salvo of naval artillery shells or missiles, but that didn't stop the seamen on the upper deck launching salvos of potatoes to the enemy.

Over the next three months, HMS BACCHANTE conducted three patrols as part of the Cod War effort. The conflict ended once NATO became involved, with the 200 nautical mile territorial limit being internationally ratified and 24 British trawlers permitted to fish within that zone at any one time. At the end of the day, NATO insisted that the strategically important UK-Faroes-Iceland gap be protected and this required the cooperation of Iceland. This gap was the underwater highway, along which the Soviet nuclear submarine fleet had to transit in order to reach the Atlantic. So, yet again, Iceland won!

Chapter 35 - DOO-WAH-DIDDY-DIDDY-DUM-DIDDY-DOO!

By early May of 1976, I was no longer a Junior and had established myself as a solid member of the Communications Department. I was now shaving every day, was making a good fist of my studies for promotion and had made some fast friends in the mess. Because I was still not 18 years-old, I was not yet permitted to drink beer onboard, however, did imbibe increasingly on the frequent 'runs ashore' with the lads. Unfortunately, I did not appear to have an off switch when it came to drinking and was gaining a bit of a reputation as a fighter. I clearly had not moved too far from my Rathgael days, when the only defence to any insult, umbrage or provocation was violence. My drinking once resulted in another visit to the Captain's Table, after I returned late after a run ashore in Portsmouth. After a failed attempt to find a potential girlfriend at Joanna's Disco in Southsea, I managed to find my way back to the dockyard. I showed my ID card to the gate police and started the long walk to Fountain Lake Jetty. Eventually, I drunkenly staggered up the gangway and felt my way down to the mess, before getting undressed and falling into a drunken sleep. I was awakened sometime later by daylight coming through a hatch. This was unusual, as my mess was two decks down and hadn't seen genuine daylight since the ship was built. I became aware of a terrible smell, something akin to rotten eggs. My eyes became accustomed to the darkness and it dawned upon me that I wasn't where I thought I was. I scrambled around trying to find my clothes.

If You Can't Take a Joke...

My T-shirt felt slimy, nevertheless I slid it over my body. I found my shoes, but my trousers eluded me. I could see from the illuminated dial on my watch that it was 7.45am and I was supposed to be back onboard by 8.00am for the morning briefing, called 'both watches', on the flight deck. I reasoned that I could not be too far from my ship, so the trouser hunt was abandoned in favour of making it back to the ship on time. I climbed a greasy ladder and found myself standing on the deck of a fueling barge. The smell of rotten eggs was actually fuel oil. I looked around, hoping desperately that I was in the vicinity of HMS BACCHANTE. Sadly, I was not. It appears that I had wandered in a drunken stupor round and round in circles and ended up on the fueling jetty, just yards from the dockyard gate – at least a 20-minute walk to Fountain Lake Jetty. I started to run. Out of breath and sweating profusely, a few minutes later I could see the ship about 100 yards away and for a brief, optimistic moment, I truly believed I was going to make it. I did not! From 50-yards away, I heard the ship's tannoy announce 'colours' – the morning tradition of raising the White Ensign on the stern of the ship. This meant that everyone was mustered and ready for the day's briefing. By this time, I had admitted defeat and had slowed to a walk, hoping that by the time I reached the ship, the crew would have been dismissed and sent off to work. Perhaps in the mass of bodies leaving the flight deck for various parts of the ship would provide me some cover and I could sneak back onboard unnoticed. Then, one of the crew spotted me on the jetty. Covered with thick, slimy oil, sweating like a sinner in confession and without trousers, my appearance inspired him to welcome me back in song, so with a distinct lack of restraint, he laughed, pointed and started singing,

"HERE HE COMES, JUST A-WALKING DOWN THE STREET, SINGING…!"

By the time he reached the end of that line, another score of sailors had joined him at the flight deck railings and joined him,

"DOO-WAH-DIDDY-DIDDY-DUM-DIDDY-DOO!"

The chorus-line increased as more and more sailors were drawn by the kerfuffle.

"SNAPPIN' HIS FINGERS AND SHUFFLING HIS FEET, SINGING DOO-WAH-DIDDY-DIDDY-DUM-DIDDY-DOO!"

I decided that the game was up, so I might as well enjoy it. I puffed out my chest, put a huge grin on my face, marched the last 30-yards and all the way up the gangway in time to my own personal soundtrack,

"HE LOOKS GOOD, HE LOOKS FINE, I THINK HE'S LOST HIS FUCKING MIND, SINGING DOO-WAH-DIDDY-DIDDY-DUM-DIDDY-DOO!"

Even the Officer of the Day, personally greeted me at the top of the gangway,

"Welcome home, RO Skull. Eleven o'clock, Captain's Table!"

As it turned out, the Captain had witnessed the whole thing and declared that, as I had done so much to improve ship's morale that morning, he would let me off with a warning. To permanently document this incident, my Divisional Officer made a note in my official record:

> **(NOTE: ANY ADV[...] [...]CTS OF [...] [...]ING'S CHA[R...]
> POWER TO REMED[Y...] IMPROVE, MUST BE UNDERL[...]**
>
> Name.... SKULL John Richard............................
>
> HMS.... BACCHANTE ....Date of Joinin[g]
> Rating.... RO2(T) .... Occasion for
>
> **SECTION I (Comments must substantiate markings in Sections II and III.)**
>
> He is perhaps the most renown member of the department in the ship - not by any means for his professional brilliance or devotion to duty but because of the compelling nature of his Irish blarney.
>
> Technically he is above average at tactical operating with a good morse speed. His biggest fault is a reluctance to admit to his own ignorance or error, or to call on more experienced advice. For his length of service he has a good grasp of naval organisation though is rather behind with his own self discipline. The fact that he managed to lose his trousers inside Portsmouth dockyard should be recorded somewhere. He believes in experimenting in life and remains willing to try anything, some of his escapades bringing him close to serious trouble.
>
> Date 5/12/76 ... Signature of Div. Officer. ...

Don't judge...I was still only 17!

This was not the only incident of note and I was, to use a naval analogy, often 'sailing too close to the wind', as is indicated in my personnel report for that year.

The next few weeks saw the ship cleaned, scraped, painted and polished to within an inch of its life in preparation for our upcoming visit to New York. We were to be a part of the largest international flotilla of warships since World War II, which was to rendezvous on the Hudson River in New York City to help with the American's bicentennial celebrations. The average age of the crew of a Leander-class frigate was about 20-years old, with plenty of teenaged matelots bringing that average significantly down. The excitement of a trip to the Big Apple was tangible and as our departure date, the 14th June approached, it was time for one last run ashore in Portsmouth. As young men, our priorities were clear – beer and women, not necessarily in that order. As luck would have it, the 12th of June was a Saturday – prime time. Each Royal Naval Dockyard had its own well-trodden path from pub to pub, before finally arriving at the final call, the hunting ground, the possibility of 'trapping' a local girl – that great 1970s institution, the Disco. In Chatham it was Scamps, in Plymouth – Diamond Lil's and in Portsmouth, it was Joanna's Disco.

Clubs and Discos were notorious for charging extortionate sums for alcohol, so it was important to get the 'beer goggles' sorted before arriving at the club. This meant stops along the way, including, The Ship and Castle, The Ship Anson, The Keppel's Head, and The Lady Hamilton, all of which were within 200 yards of each other. The unwritten rules of the run ashore were simple:

- Pubs are for your mates
- Discos and clubs for mating
- If your mate has made contact, that girl is out of bounds to you
- If your mate is making headway and his 'prospect' has a friend, you are honour-bound to act as wingman, regardless of her friend's potential

- If your mate has told her he is the ship's helicopter pilot, he's the bloody helicopter pilot!

By the time we reached Joanna's, there were only three in our little group – myself, Nobby Hall and Scouse Liddle. This was somewhat awkward, as most girls were in pairs or quartets and this severely hampered our mission. We ordered our pints and made our way to the edge of the dancefloor, where we had to keep shuffling our feet, lest we end up glued to the sticky carpet. The heady combination of cigarette smoke, the rancid carpet and stale body odour overwhelmed the eyes and taste buds. The volume of the music vibrated my fillings and restricted communication to sign and body language. It was almost impossible to ask a girl to dance, so the routine was to simply move to her spot on the dancefloor, start dancing and try to make eye contact. There were three potential outcomes. If she smiled and started moving with you, that was good. If she ignored you and turned away, that was fairly normal and you had to take the long walk of rejection and shame back to your mates. The third, and least favourable, outcome was that you hadn't realized that she was with her boyfriend, who'd just gone to get the next round of drinks and that could be bad.

Nobby, Scouse and I had pretty much resigned ourselves to failure, a taxi and a burger from the van outside the dockyard gate, when suddenly Nobby's eyes lit up. He nudged us and flicked his head towards the dancefloor. There, in flagrant disregard of the long tradition of the Disco, were three girls dancing together. It was getting late, so strategy at this point was paramount. First, we had to decide who would be dancing with whom. We were all slightly tipsy, in our teens, hornier than an 8-point moose and had not even spoken to these girls. It turned out that we all wanted to dance with the same girl and it wasn't because of her sparkling personality. After further sign language, we worked it out. The next challenge was when to make our move. As it was getting close to the house lights coming on, the edges of the dancefloor was becoming more crowded with other equally desperate young men, so timing was crucial. Too early and you could find yourself having to buy them a drink, but too late and others could make their move first. The final consideration was the inevitable slow dances that always rounded off the Disco. When the slow songs start and a girl isn't already dancing with someone, she will just leave the dancefloor. Girls getting their groove on together to KC and the Sunshine's Band's and singing along, *"That's the way, uh-huh uh-huh, I like it"* is acceptable, however, they have nowhere to go but home, if the next song is Lionel Ritchie's belly-rubbing classic, "Three Times a Lady". Our timing was immaculate and before you could say "Heaven Must Be Missing an Angel", we joined the trio of dancing girls, received smiles of acceptance or perhaps they were grimaces of resignation that we three were the best they could expect so close to midnight. Soon, I was slow dancing with my girl in the standard 1970s position – my arms around her waist and hers around my neck. The music volume now low enough to hear each other and I found out that her name was Valerie, she was 18-years-old and lived with her mother. Bummer. When the lights finally came up after about three songs, I was relieved to see that Valerie was an attractive young woman, with a friendly smile and easy laugh. As the Disco closed, we were herded out onto the street, like toothpaste being extruded from a tube. We searched in vain for Nobby, Scouse and Val's friends, Angie and Liz, but to no avail. Val told me that Angie and Liz shared a flat in Southsea and had probably taken the boys home with them. I had to settle for a quick snog in the doorway of the Intrepid Bun burger joint, before hailing down a taxi to take Val home……alone. I had told her that I was sailing to the States on Monday, so we exchanged addresses and promised to write.

Chapter 36 – Gibraltar Sun, Sea and Sand

I was enjoying the happiest time of my life. I wasn't yet 18-years-old, but felt grown up. I had a career, money in my pocket and I was about to sail to America with my friends. Clearly, I'd had some minor disciplinary problems, but was learning that if you worked hard and contributed to the overall success of your team, these indiscretions were quickly forgiven and forgotten. I had pushed the memories of Bawnmore and Rathgael into the deepest recesses of my mind and I was determined not to let my horrendous childhood experiences dictate the sort of person I wanted to be. I had spent only a few months in the family home in England and it was nearly 18-months since I had left there to join the Royal Navy, so I hadn't had enough time to get close to my mother and siblings. Occasionally, I would spend a weekend at the house in Ferndown, but everyone seemed to move around me as if I was just a temporary hindrance, like a

If You Can't Take a Joke...

pensioner at the checkout counting all her small coins, while you tap your foot impatiently. I really could not wait to go back to my home in HMS BACCHANTE on Sunday evenings. I did not miss my family, they did not miss me and that was fine.

HMS BACCHANTE's first port-of-call on our voyage to the USA, was Gibraltar, or Gib for short, a jewel in the British Crown and a mote in the eye of the Spaniard. In 1976, the Spanish had closed the land border with Gibraltar, so we were limited to our little corner of the Empire. The territory is only three miles long and just over a mile at its widest point and is of huge strategic value. The Strait of Gibraltar, only nine miles wide, is the gateway to the Mediterranean and has always been of great value both militarily and commercially. The town itself is only around ninety acres, sits in the northwest corner and is conveniently located adjacent to the dockyard. There were often as many as six warships in port and with permanent Navy, Army and Air Force personnel numbering in the thousands, ninety acres may seem pretty cramped. However, within that small area, Gibraltar boasted 365 bars – one for every day of the year.

As part of ensuring that everything would be at the high standard required for us to represent our country in New York, every nook and cranny of the ship was inspected. The crew had to dig out our white tropical uniforms and were paraded and inspected by our various Divisional Officers. One of our seamen, Zac, was of Jamaican heritage and carried his blackness proudly. As he was being inspected, his Divisional Officer appeared to be dissatisfied with the standard of shine on Zac's shoes,

If You Can't Take a Joke...

"This isn't good enough. Are these your best shoes?"

Zac looked somewhat puzzled,

"My best shoes, sir?"

"Yes, your best shoes. You're supposed to wear your best shoes on parade!"

"Can't, sir."

The Divisional Offer was starting to get a little irate,

"Can't? What do you mean? Why can't you wear your best shoes?"

Zac, in the broadest Jamaican accent he could muster, replied,

"My best shoes, sir...... they're green suede!"

After the briefest moment of complete silence, the whole parade, including the inspecting officer burst into laughter. There was clearly no hope of recovering the situation, so the officer quickly decided,

"PARADE......DISMISSED!"

We were only in Gibraltar for a short time, primarily to store ship, top up our fuel and, importantly take on a few hundred thousand US dollars in cash. It was standard practice for the Supply Officer and his team to dish out local currency prior to entering each new port of call. A form was sent to each messdeck and the mess members would specify how much cash they would need. These were the days before ATMs, ready availability of credit or debit cards, so cash was king. This was not an issue in Gibraltar, as their currency was good old Sterling. However, this did not stop rogue memos reaching messdecks offering currency exchange from Sterling to 'Gibloons', just to catch out the new boys.

I had one free day in Gibraltar and wanted to experience the local culture, rather than just sit around in bars. Gib had the reputation of being just about the hardest port in the Mediterranean to 'meet' women, because it was a very Roman Catholic community, so expectations were that any run ashore would simply be a drinking, joking and bonding session for the lads. I had done quite enough drinking and bonding in the recent past and was desperately trying to avoid any repetition of the 'sans trousers' episode or unplanned visits to the Captain's Table, so set off with my camera and headed into town.

This was my first real independent experience of life in a truly different environment. When I visited Amsterdam on HMS JUNO a few months earlier, I was still very much a trainee and conscious of the fact that I was under continuous scrutiny. Also, in my youthful perspective, I didn't see much of a difference in the culture of Amsterdam compared to cities in England. To me, the Dutch were just like the English, except for the language. Gibraltar was different. The locals spoke English, but gone was the greyness of northern Europe. It was the height of the summer and the levant winds from the Eastern Mediterranean brought hot, sunny weather, so I headed to Catalan Beach for a bit of swimming and sun-worshiping. This was the 1970s, so instead of applying sun protection in the form of SPF50 sunscreen, the norm was to baste oneself in coconut oil. This would be re-applied until you smelled like a Piña Colada and could hear your skin crackling. I'm from Northern Ireland, so my natural skin tone is best described as Azure White, tending towards pale blue and not long after my short run across the sandy beach and a dip in the warm Mediterranean Sea, most of the coconut oil had washed off. I lay back down on my towel, closed my eyes and daydreamed of my American adventures to come. Sadly, these daydreams soon turned into proper sleep-dreams, as the combination of gentle levant breeze and warming sun lulled me into a deep sleep. I estimate that I roasted for about two hours at around Gas Mark 4, before I finally woke up. I could feel my whole body burning up, but when I looked all the way down my now shrimp-pink body to my feet, I was horrified. The tops of my feet were fiery red, swollen and blistered. As I stood up and put on my T-shirt and shorts, I felt every grain of sand etching my whole body and realized that there was no way any sort of footwear could adorn my feet. There was no transport from Catalan Bay to the dockyard, so I had a barefoot one-and-a-half-mile walk ahead of me. Fortunately, I would be in shade for a fair portion, as my route included the Admiralty Tunnel, which runs directly east-west through the middle of the Rock of Gibraltar. I was in pretty poor shape, with the constant stinging of sunburn, the increasing pain in my feet and dehydration. Halfway along the tunnel, thankfully, was the Gibraltar Communications Centre. I pressed the buzzer at the security gate and after showing my ID card was allowed in. All I really wanted was some water to drink, but when the Duty Petty Officer saw the state of me, he immediately stuck me under a cold shower and ordered me to stay there. It was heaven.

Phone calls were made, transport arranged and within an hour, I was tucked in bed in the ship's Sick Bay and covered completely in

If You Can't Take a Joke…

ointment. My feet were bandaged and I was pumped with painkillers. The Medic had contacted my Divisional Officer and told him I would not be able to work for a couple of days. I was still in the Sick Bay bed, when we left harbour and started our trans-Atlantic crossing. I was hugely disappointed not to be at my station on the bridge, but a couple of my messmates visited me and Butch even managed to smuggle me a tin of beer to help with the rehydration.

A couple of days later, I also received a visit from the Master-at-Arms,

"How are you feeling, RO Skull?" he asked gently.

"Not too bad, Master. The Medic says I can go back to the mess in the morning."

"Oh, that is good news. Will you be able to wear shoes?" he asked.

"Yep, all good, Master." I replied happily.

"GOOD, 'COS YOU'RE GOING TO NEED THEM TO MARCH TO CAPTAIN'S FUCKING TABLE!" he shouted.

I was confused,

"Captain's table…what for?"

"YOU'RE BEING CHARGED WITH ABSENCE FROM DUTY BY WAY OFF SELF-INFLICTED INJURY, YOU DOZY SOD!"

Bugger.

Chapter 37 – Welcome to America Y'all!

Prior to the big show in New York, HMS BACCHANTE spent a few days in Wilmington, Delaware. Not only did this visit afford us the necessary time to make our final preparations for the big event in New York, it also helped acclimatize us to the United States of America, her people and culture. All we knew of America was what we gleaned from the movies and television. If anything, I was an avid viewer of Bonanza, Little House on the Prairie and Happy Days, so Wilmington wasn't too great a culture shock. It is a small city, about 30 miles and 30 years from Philadelphia, with friendly people and a small-town feel. The ship was open to visitors and we took it in turns to show families around our great Royal Navy ship. Without exception, local families offered all the sailors who conducted these tours some level of hospitality. This generosity did not just extend to a home-cooked meal, but everything except legal adoption. They took us on tours to see performances at the Grand Opera House and to family BBQs along the Delaware riverwalk. Many of the crew took advantage of the Americans fascination with anything English, with HMS BACCHANTE caps, T-shirts and other items of uniform ending up adorning many of the women of Wilmington. By the time we left Wilmington, we collected local newspaper reports, which included headline, such as:

- **THIRSTY BRITISH DRAIN CITY PUBS!**
- **BRITISH SAILORS MISSING IN RED MUSTANG!**

The last headline related to two young sailors who apparently fell deeply in lust with a couple of local girls. They were eventually picked up by local police and returned to the ship.

I felt overwhelmed by the lifestyle and kindness of the people of Wilmington. There was an openness, which told me that it did not matter where I came from, how I spoke or my lowly status onboard. They liked my sense of humour, enjoyed my Irish-ness and treated me like a friend. They didn't mind when I got a little drunk and kept me safe. America in the mid-70s was the place to be, wasn't it?

All too soon, we had to bid farewell to our new friends in Wilmington and sail north to New York City, which was only a day's steaming away. As we left, the quayside was a throng of cheering and waving people, some of whom, mainly young women, had arranged to travel to New York to continue bonding and bonking their new British buddies.

Chapter 38 – Happy 200th, America!

Given the prominence of the International Naval Review and the Bicentennial celebrations, our entry into the city, on 3 July, had been coordinated to the second. The event saw the largest and longest fleet review in New York history, with over 6 million people watching from the shores of the Hudson River and millions more following on national television. More than 50 warships from 30 countries began in the pre-dawn as the United States Navy guided missile cruiser Constitution passed under the Verrazano-Narrows bridge and fired a 21-gun salute, with the boom travelling across the bay all the way up to New York City. Like every ship in the formation, our crew were dressed in our best tropical white uniformed and lined the guardrails around the whole ship. My station was on the signal deck, which afforded possibly the best viewing platform on the ship. It was a beautiful, sunny morning and pleasure and anticipation fueled the excited chatter amongst the sailors. As the 21-gun salute was returned by an artillery battery on shore, we could hear the cheers of the crowd. Ships from Japan, Norway, Spain, the United Kingdom, Australia, Brazil, Italy and many more steamed north towards the city and it took over four hours for the whole flotilla to pass under the starting point. It seemed that anyone in New York and New Jersey who had a boat was on the river that day. In a break from tradition, we were given permission to relax our rigid 'attention' stance to return the waves and shouts until we got closer to Manhattan Island. I could already see the Manhattan skyline, until then just an image from the movies, and it

If You Can't Take a Joke…

took my breath away. Look at me, I thought, the guttersnipe from Belfast in fucking New York City! I was on the starboard side of the ship and just managed a quick glimpse of the Statue of Liberty, before we altered course to take us towards our turning point at George Washington Bridge, where we would turn around and steam back south to our berth at one of the piers on 12th Avenue, close to West 54th Street. Finally alongside in New York City, we were dismissed from our posts and headed down to the messdecks to get ready for the run ashore. I was on the Duty Watch that evening, so had to watch enviously as Butch, Nobby, Scouse and the rest of my friends head off into the city. However, this also meant that I was definitely not stuck onboard the next night, the big night, the best night.

July 4th, 1976 and I was going to help America celebrate its 200th birthday. By 10.00am, it was estimated that there were around 30,000 pleasure craft packed into the harbour, most at maximum passenger capacity, if not more. News helicopters buzzed overhead, vying for the best pictures. The main roads in Manhattan leading down to the riverside were blocked to vehicle traffic and a throng of hundreds of thousands moved along like ants. The formal festivities began with a procession of sixteen of the world's last remaining tall-ships entering the harbour and sailing up the river. The Gods of wind were generous that day, with just enough breeze to fill the sails of the tall-ships and providing a spectacle that would never be forgotten by the millions of onlookers gathered on the shore. They were on the waterfront, perched in trees, peering out of skyscraper windows, anywhere to witness this historic moment. The best view, by far, was from the

If You Can't Take a Joke...

giant United States Navy aircraft carrier, the USS Forrestal, from where the salute was taken by President Gerald Ford, accompanied by Vice President Nelson Rockefeller. At exactly 2.00pm, the President rang the ship's bell and officially signaled a national 2-minute bell ring. The impact was immediate in Manhattan and the ringing of every bell, from Cathedrals, churches, fire stations and even bicycles once again brought waves of cheering and clapping from the millions of spectators. It was the most astonishing thing I'd ever witnessed and I was impatient to get ashore and be part of the story.

Soon enough, it was 4.00pm and I was finally off-duty. I gathered in the mess with the lads and again someone gave me a cheeky couple of beers to whet the whistle, so to speak. Before we could go ashore, we had to have the obligatory 'chat' from the First Lieutenant about the dangers of our new city and, in particular, which areas we should avoid. On this occasion, we also had a guest speaker, a New York-Irish police captain, who had seen 25-years' service under his belt, which in turn looked like it has just seen 25 donuts. It appeared that all his experience had not taught him anything about young British men, as everything he said was greet by howls of laughter,

"Now, the legal age for drinking in New York is 21-years, so you won't want to be drinking, will you?" was his hilarious opener. Even before the laughter died down, he continued,

"Our wonderful city has plenty of interesting places to visit, like the Empire State Building, the Statue of Liberty and the Guggenheim Museum. Much more fun than getting drunk and rowdy, yes?" He continued in this vein for some minutes, when the First Lieutenant realized that his approach was perhaps more suited to high school students than this motley crew, so he interrupted,

"Captain, could you perhaps advise the crew about which areas are best avoided?"

In defence of the First Lieutenant, we were all very aware that at that time, New York was very much a city in turmoil. US economic torpor in the early '70s hit New York City particularly hard and a large exodus of middle-class residents to the suburbs drained the city of tax revenue. Just a year before our visit, the city had run out of money to pay for normal operating expenses and narrowly escaped bankruptcy. The city had the highest incidents of police corruption, drug dealing, muggings, prostitution, rape and murder in the United States and I was about to go for a 'run ashore'. The police captain seemed uncertain or unwilling to address the First Lieutenant's question, so simply responded,

"I've left a copy of the latest tourist information for each member of the crew. I suggest you read it carefully. Have a nice day!"

True to his word, as we left the flight deck to go below to make our final personal preparations for the night out, I picked up a copy of the brochure. It made interesting reading! The following extracts are taken directly from the brochure:

- **Stay off the streets after 6pm** – Even in midtown Manhattan, muggings and occasional murders are on the increase
- **Do not walk** – If you must leave your hotel after 6pm, summon a taxi or ask your doorman to call one

- **Avoid public transport** – Subway crime is so high that the City recently had to close off the rear half of trains so that the public could huddle together for safety

> **WELCOME TO FEAR CITY**
> A Survival Guide for Visitors to the City of New York
>
> The incidence of crime and violence in New York City is shockingly high, and is getting worse every day. During the four month period ended Apr. 30, 1975, robberies were up 21%; aggravated assault was up 15%; larceny was up 22%; and burglary was up 19%.
> Now, to "solve" his budget problems, Mayor Beame is going to discharge substantial numbers of firefighters and law enforcement officers of all kinds. By the time you read this, the number of public safety personnel available to protect residents and visitors may already have been still further reduced. Under those circumstances, the best advice we can give you is this: Until things change, stay away from New York City if you possibly can.
> Nevertheless, some New Yorkers do manage to survive and even to keep their property intact. The following guidelines have been prepared by a council of firefighters and law officers to help you enjoy your visit to the City of New York in comfort and safety.
>
> Good luck.
>
> **1.** **Stay off the streets after 6 P.M.** Even in midtown Manhattan, muggings and occasional murders are on the increase during the early evening hours. Do not be misled by the late sunsets during the summer season. If you walk in midtown at about 7:30 P.M., you will observe that the streets are nearly deserted.
>
> **2.** **Do not walk.** If you must leave your hotel after 6 P.M., try not to go out alone. Summon a radio taxi by telephone, or ask the hotel doorman to call a taxi while you remain in the hotel lobby. Follow the same procedure when leaving the restaurant, theatre, or other location of your evening activity.

There was a separate sheet from the First Lieutenant proposing that we avoid known crime hotspots, mainly Harlem and the Bronx. To us these were the names from TV and movies and conjured up images of cool dudes, hip clothes and playing that funky music 'til we died. Not only that, it was bloody walking distance from the ship!

I was going ashore with my usual little gang – myself, Nobby and Scouse. We inspected ourselves, before heading down the gangway. We looked awesome in our crisp white tropical uniforms, pocketsful of Yankee dollars and liberally splashed with Paco Rabanne. How

If You Can't Take a Joke…

could the girls of New York City resist? We saw ourselves as the three sailors in the old movie, 'On the Town', starring Frank Sinatra, Gene Kelly and that other guy who everyone forgets. Usually on a run ashore, the first stop is the bar closest to the ship. That night, however, there was to be somewhere in the region of 25,000 sailors from 30 countries helping the locals to celebrate. Even though it was a Sunday, there was a carnival atmosphere, with food stalls, buskers and other street performers aplenty. The New York Police Department were also out in force, but there were no signs of the social unrest we'd been advised about. That day, it appeared that everyone was just happy to be in New York City. The nearest five bars to the piers were packed to the rafters with sailors, at various stages of intoxication, so we kept moving north. We knew that NYC could easily swallow up the myriad of matelots on the town that night, but we had to get further away from the ships. It was a warm, sunny evening, so we decided, despite the dire warnings of the NYPD Captain, to head to Harlem by way of a stroll through Central Park.

Late at night, Central Park was indeed a very scary place, but in the early evening of 4th July 1976, it was Party Central Park. In addition to the many official activities, families, groups of friends and impromptu gatherings of all descriptions were singing, dancing and drinking. Our blindingly white uniforms were like beacons and Nobby, Scouse and I had barely set foot in the park before welcoming beers were thrust upon us. Whereabouts in England are you from? What do you think of America? Have you met the Queen? We loved being the centre of attention, particularly as there was free beer involved. We'd stay with the group long enough to be polite, before making our excuses and heading off in a northerly direction. Harlem was only about two miles distant, but looking at the throngs of party-goers in the park, we realized we probably weren't going to make it there, so we settled in for an evening of outdoor hospitality from our American cousins. Dinner was the biggest hotdog I'd ever seen from a stand advertising "Voted the Best Hotdog in NYC". I stepped up to the Hot Dog Stand and committed my first cultural faux pas of the trip,

"Can I just have a plain hotdog, please?"

The vendor, a proper New Yorker, looked at me as if I had two heads,

"First time in New York, huh? Look, pal, it's my 200th birthday and you need a proper 'dog… you need da woiks, right?"

"Sorry, what's 'da woiks'?"

"Y'know, chilli, onions, cheese……da woiks!"

"Oh, the works!"

"Dats what I'm sayin', da woiks! Okay, one woiks comin' right up! Dat'll be a dolla', pal."

After a couple of minutes of tonging, spooning and pouring, he passed me my order. I handed him one of my crisp $5 bills,

"Thanks, mate, and Happy Birthday!"

He looked at me with a huge New York City smile,

"Well, dat's most kind. You have a nice day now, y'hear!"

He kept the change, but that wasn't the end of the hotdog adventure! At that point in the evening, we had been grabbed and were being hosted by three very attractive girls, who were thrilled by our uniforms, our accents and the fact that we had some cash. We had been buying them drinks for a couple of hours from the numerous liquor stands that had been especially licenced for the celebrations. Things were going swimmingly. I returned to the group with da woiks and sat down on the grass beside my new friend, Pam. I lifted my hotdog, which resembled a train crash, and sunk my teeth into it. Then physics took over. As I compressed the end of the hotdog, it altered the hydrodynamics of the whole bun and the chilli, onion and cheese sauce slid off the bun and into my lap – my crisp, white, starched lap. With a sort of squeal, Pamela grabbed a bottle of water and quickly doused my trousers and started frantically rubbing and dabbing at my groinage, in a frantic attempt to limit the damage. After a few seconds of her desperate rubbing, the chilli stain became secondary in my concerns. To that point, my sexual experience had been limited to running away from a prostitute in Harwich, failing miserably with a prostitute in Amsterdam and a snog in the doorway of The Intrepid Bun in Southsea. I was very much still cherry-intacto and was becoming increasingly desperate to pop it! However, early evening in the middle of Central Park, with a girl I had just met, was possibly not the appropriate time, place nor person for my manhood to suddenly present himself. To be fair, though, Pamela was doing the rubbing, not me! I was mortified, but she just raised one eyebrow and suggested,

"I think I should take you home and get you out of those wet things!"

If You Can't Take a Joke...

We had given up on ever making it to Harlem, given the size of the crowds, so Pam and I agreed to meet up with them later in the evening in Times Square. We knew the crowds would be equally formidable, so Pam arranged a specific meeting point at 10.00pm. Knowing glances passed between Scouse and Nobby, as I wandered off with Pam. She was older than me and at 23-years-old, much more sophisticated. She was born and raised in NYC, studied journalism in college there and at that time had an internship at one of the daily newspapers. She was beautiful, intelligent and funny, whereas I was skinny, clumsy and funny looking. This is not Fifty Shades of Grey, so I shall spare you the finer details, so let's just say that while my stained trousers were spinning in the washing machine, my head was spinning for very different reasons. POP!

By the time my trousers had dried, we were too late to make our rendezvous in Times Square, so we stayed in, drank beer, smoked a little weed and Pam continued my education. Happy Birthday, indeed!

If You Can't Take a Joke...

Chapter 39 – All Grown Up

We enjoyed another couple of days in New York, readied for sea and set course across the Atlantic for Portsmouth. We managed to lose a couple of crew members, who had obviously succumbed to the razzle and dazzle of the United States. They never did return to HMS BACCHANTE, so I like to imagine them getting by on their British charm and their accents. Just after we left New York, the ship had received news that our program for the next few months had changed again. If you can't take a joke, you shouldn't have joined! In this case, however, it was all good news. After a few weeks in UK, we would be sailing again in August and our itinerary was amazing. We were to head south into the Mediterranean, with stops in Lisbon and good old Gibraltar. Then to the Eastern Med, through the Suez Canal and south to Mombasa for a two-week maintenance period, which would allow the opportunity for a few wives and girlfriends to join their men in sunny Kenya. After this, we would head east into the Indian Ocean for a visit to Karachi, before starting the long cruise back to Portsmouth, via Bahrain, Alexandria and Gib. The crew were delighted with this news and I was beside myself with excitement. HMS BACCHANTE was sailing back to the UK unaccompanied, so there were no exercises, no massive preparations for special events, just around 10 days quietly cruising in the summer calm of the Atlantic.

In the six months I had been part of the crew, I had proved myself worthy of my position in the team, more than that actually, a valued member of the team. My ready sense of humour won me friends, not only in my messdeck, but also throughout the ship. I was working hard on my promotion exams, performing my duties enthusiastically and my confidence level was right where it needed to be. I would be eighteen in a month or so and I was nailing life. Bawnmore, Rathgael, Judge Bailey, the bullies, the cruel staff and my childhood trials and tribulations were well behind me.

I would go on to enjoy rapid promotion through the ranks and at 29 years old gain a commission to the officer ranks. I served in the Royal Navy for 21 years, during which time, I assisted in crushing the might of the Soviet Empire, defeating the dastardly Argentinian junta and saving the mighty British Cod from the evil undersized nets of those Icelandic fish-pirates. Not bad for a guttersnipe from Belfast!

Epilogue - Historical Institutional Abuse (Northern Ireland) Enquiry

The Inquiry was independent from government and had two main components. One was the Acknowledgement Forum, whose members listened to the experiences of those who were children in residential institutions (other than schools) in Northern Ireland between 1922 and 1995.

The other component was the Statutory Inquiry. In its 223 days of public hearings between 13 January 2014 and 8 July 2016 it investigated 22 institutions, as well as the circumstances surrounding the sending of child migrants from Northern Ireland to Australia, and the activities of Fr Brendan Smyth, and issues of finance and governance. The cost of the Enquiry was £10.74M and the final report was released in January 2017. The following criticisms were generally common to all institutes covered by the Enquiry:

- The use of frequent unrecorded informal corporal punishment was unacceptable and amounted to systemic abuse.
- The Welfare Authorities throughout Northern Ireland failed to ensure that institutes were inspected for up to 15 years was a systemic failing.
- The extent of the unregulated physical punishment applied by some staff amounted to systemic abuse.
- The failure to prevent bullying by peers amounted to systemic abuse.

- The lack of training in control and restraint was a systemic failing.
- Staff routinely failed to report physical, emotional and sexual abuse of residents to either their superiors or the relevant authorities – a systematic failing.

A number of staff members and 'visitors' to institutions have been prosecuted and imprisoned for physical and sexual abuse offences committed against children in their care. Sadly, many of those who, as children, suffered throughout their lives, because of the treatment they received in Bawnmore Boys' Home and Rathgael Training School. I know that at least two of my small circle of childhood friends committed suicide and others have been unable to work, suffer mental health issues and survive on welfare benefits. Compensation may provide a little comfort, but it will never erase the memories.

Printed in Poland
by Amazon Fulfillment
Poland Sp. z o.o., Wrocław
12 June 2022

5e49080b-9a49-4ff1-b449-0bbada0e8624R01